DATE DUE

May 11			
GAYLORD			PRINTED IN U.S.A.

Headline Series

No. 280　　**FOREIGN POLICY ASSOCIATION**　　$4.00

Presidents, Public Opinion and Power

The Nixon, Carter and Reagan Years
by Terry L. Deibel

Introduction　3

1
Power and Public Opinion
in the Post-Vietnam Era　5

2
Nixon, Kissinger and Geopolitics　20

3
Jimmy Carter,
Denial of Power
and the Quest for Values　33

4
Reagan and the Restoration
of American Power　48

5
Public Opinion
and the Policy Triangle　62

Talking It Over　70
Reading List　71

Cover Design: Hersch Wartik

Sept./Oct. 1986
Published April 1987.

The Author

TERRY L. DEIBEL is professor of national security policy at the National War College in Washington, D.C., where he teaches a course on foreign policy memoirs from the Carter and Nixon Administrations. Dr. Deibel received his Ph.D. from the Fletcher School of Law and Diplomacy, Tufts University. He has also taught international affairs at the Georgetown University School of Foreign Service, and served in the Office of Management and Budget and the Department of State. He is the
author of numerous articles on foreign policy and international affairs. Most recently he concentrated on American security commitments in the Third World during a year at the Carnegie Endowment for International Peace in Washington, D.C.

The Foreign Policy Association

The Foreign Policy Association is a private, nonprofit, nonpartisan educational organization. Its purpose is to stimulate wider interest and more effective participation in, and greater understanding of, world affairs among American citizens. Among its activities is the continuous publication, dating from 1935, of the HEADLINE SERIES. The author is responsible for factual accuracy and for the views expressed. FPA itself takes no position on issues of U.S. foreign policy.

HEADLINE SERIES (ISSN 0017-8780) is published five times a year, January, March, May, September and November, by the Foreign Policy Association, Inc., 205 Lexington Ave., New York, N.Y. 10016. Chairman, Robert V. Lindsay; President, John W. Kiermaier; Editor in Chief, Nancy L. Hoepli; Senior Editor, Ann R. Monjo; Associate Editor, K. M. Rohan. Subscription rates, $15.00 for 5 issues; $25.00 for 10 issues; $30.00 for 15 issues. Single copy price $4.00. Discount 25% on 10 to 99 copies; 30% on 100 to 499; 35% on 500 to 999; 40% on 1,000 or more. Payment must accompany order for $8 or less. Add $1 for postage. Second-class postage paid at New York, N.Y. POSTMASTER: Send address changes to HEADLINE SERIES, Foreign Policy Association, 205 Lexington Ave., New York, N.Y. 10016. Copyright 1987 by Foreign Policy Association, Inc. Composed and printed at Science Press, Ephrata, Pennsylvania.

Library of Congress Catalog Card No. 87-80536
ISBN 0-87124-112-9

Charts on pp. 12, 17 and 65 by Robert Mansfield. Cover photos: Mt. Rushmore, UPI/Bettmann Newsphotos; President Reagan, N.Y. Public Library Picture Collection.

Introduction

The past two decades have been a period of great turmoil in U.S. foreign policy. From Vietnam to Grenada and from MX to SDI, from Bretton Woods to floating exchange rates and from world creditor to world debtor, from the Nixon Doctrine to the Reagan Doctrine and from oil shortages to oil glut, from Mao Zedong to Deng Xiaoping and from Brezhnev to Gorbachev—Americans have been on a roller coaster of change in their world relationships. Not surprisingly, there have been substantial shifts in their foreign policy preferences, and they have elected such different Presidents as Richard M. Nixon, Jimmy Carter and Ronald Reagan. Responding to internal pressures and coping with chaotic external events, these men in turn have offered three quite distinct foreign policy prescriptions that go far to define the universe of likely American approaches to the world in the years immediately ahead.

This HEADLINE SERIES attempts to understand these recent shifts in American foreign policy. Changes both within the United States and in its external environment have made the post-Vietnam era a far more difficult period for American foreign policy than the two decades following World War II. Three broad foreign policy approaches have been tried during this era—those of the Nixon-Ford (Kissinger), Carter and Reagan Administrations. It is worthwhile to look not only at their failures but especially at what each has offered that might be of enduring value in constructing a stable and viable post-Reagan foreign policy.

Of course, the effort to summarize in so broad a fashion presents many hazards. Though they take their character from their commanders in chief, Administrations are hardly single-minded in foreign policy matters. They are composed of a variety of officials with differing ideas about policy, so one Administration can speak with different, even opposed, voices. Nor can foreign policy be adequately characterized by reference to just a few lines of endeavor; the texture of American relations with other countries is far too rich and deep, and much of it remains unchanged in spite of the broad political thrusts of each new Administration. Then, too, an Administration and the people who compose it change over time, learning from their mistakes and altering their policies. But despite the difficulties attendant upon any generalized survey, not to attempt to make some sense of the sweep of recent American foreign policy is to forfeit the chance to learn from it.

Even though this was entirely a personal effort and represents only my own views, I wish to thank the then Commandant of the National War College, Major General Perry Smith, USAF, for providing the sabbatical year when it was written, and Thomas L. Hughes and Larry L. Fabian of the Carnegie Endowment for International Peace, where I was resident associate during its composition. Nothing in this HEADLINE SERIES should be taken as necessarily reflecting the official policy of the United States government or any of its agencies.

Terry L. Deibel
March 1987

1

Power and Public Opinion in the Post-Vietnam Era

Americans who came of age in the two decades after World War II grew used to viewing their country as a colossus on the world stage, a superpower without parallel. Their expectations of what the United States should be able to accomplish in its foreign policy remain attached to that era, as if the country could still, in the stirring words of President John F. Kennedy, "pay any price, bear any burden" for the defense of liberty everywhere.

Yet most Americans today also recognize another truth, more or less consciously. They recall the frustrations of waiting in long lines for gasoline, the searing images of a mob holding their compatriots hostage in Tehran, the helicopter, struggling free of clinging humanity, lifting off the embassy roof in Saigon. Americans understand that resources now are more limited, that uncontrollable terrorists lurk, that shiny new Hondas and Sonys add up to trade deficits in the hundreds of millions of dollars. They have seen a series of Presidents weakened by political scandal or major foreign policy disasters.

The year 1968 is as good as any to mark the shift between these perceptions of strength and vulnerability. That was the year, it will be recalled, that began with the North Korean seizure and detention of the American spy ship *Pueblo*; continued with the Tet offensive, the psychological beginning of the end of the Vietnam War; and wound up its first quarter with the decision of President Lyndon B. Johnson to withdraw from the presidential campaign of that year, a confession of new weakness in the government's executive branch. Then came the assassinations of Martin Luther King Jr. and Robert F. Kennedy, a summer of racial violence in American cities, and the tumultuous Democratic party convention in Chicago, each event signaling political instability and a lack of societal cohesion at the base of American power. Fall brought with it renewed antiwar protests on American campuses and a bitterly fought and narrowly won presidential campaign.

In retrospect it is clear that these events were symptomatic of a historic change in the United States' relative power position in world affairs. As Henry A. Kissinger later wrote:

> In the life of nations, as of human beings, a point is often reached when the seemingly limitless possibilities of youth suddenly narrow and one must come to grips with the fact that not every option is open any longer.... [W]e were becoming like other nations in the need to recognize that our power, while vast, had limits. Our resources were no longer infinite in relation to our problems; instead we had to set priorities, both intellectual and material.

The Decline of American Power

Nothing in their recent past had prepared Americans for so wrenching a change. Indeed, for more than two decades prior to 1968 the United States had enjoyed a historically unique preeminence in the global-power equation. World War II had exhausted both its new, cold-war adversaries and its industrialized allies; the United States was the only major power not devastated in that conflict. Its economy, vastly expanded as a result of the wartime effort, captured well over half of gross world production. Although quickly demobilized, American military forces were strong and modern and had control of a worldwide chain of bases from which U.S. leaders could project military power.

But a nation's power depends on more than just these concrete elements. It is also based on intangibles like domestic stability, popular support for foreign policy objectives, and the leaders' will and ability to use its power. By today's standards, U.S. national self-confidence and social cohesion after World War II were very high. The American political system was relatively disciplined and effective, with strong Presidents like Harry S. Truman, Dwight D. Eisenhower and Jack Kennedy at the helm and Congress under the sway of capable leaders like Sam Rayburn and Lyndon Johnson. People generally trusted their government. And, after an initial period of debate, American opinion leaders were generally agreed on containment of communism as the central principle of foreign policy.

In a Class by Itself

The United States, in other words, was the world's only superpower. The very term was new, reflecting the unique condition of a country, virtually without competitors, that possessed both a power base of enormous potential (in its vast territory, abundant resources, talented people, stable political system and vibrant economy) and enough of the tools necessary to conduct foreign policy (like military forces, foreign aid dollars, radio transmitters and covert action capabilities). Not only did the United States possess these sinews of power; it was *seen* as possessing them, a vitally important fact since power is at bottom a psychological phenomenon. Furthermore, the United States enjoyed great prestige, what Professor Robert Gilpin defined as the "reputation for power" and former Secretary of State Dean Acheson called "the shadow cast by power." As the leader of the coalition that had just defeated totalitarian militarism, the United States was presumed to embody the goals of much of the rest of the world and its hegemony was widely accepted.

By the late 1960s, however, many of these conditions were changing. Now largely rebuilt after the war's devastation, the Soviet Union was achieving economic growth rates consistently superior to those of the United States and was building massive military forces, both nuclear and conventional.

Competitors were arising elsewhere as well. With the help of American economic aid, the United States' industrialized allies had fully recovered from the war and begun to challenge American commercial predominance. Their economic confidence also brought with it a sense of political independence and a lessened willingness to accept American viewpoints and leadership.

By the late 1960s, too, the anticolonial movement had brought the Third World into existence. The new governments there were not controlled by docile European allies but by nationalist leaders whose determination to maintain independence meant at best a certain distance from the United States, or nonalignment, at worst anti-Americanism. Membership in the United Nations first doubled, then tripled, and the automatic pro-American majority of the 1950s vanished in a cloud of anti-imperialist rhetoric. Many of these new states were economically fragile and politically unstable. Their weaknesses demanded more American attention while providing opportunities for the exercise of growing Soviet power.

These three developments—the growth of Soviet power, the recovery of Europe and Japan, and the birth of the Third World—were *systemic* changes: broad, historic shifts in the fundamental nature of the international system that were very largely beyond American control. Though the United States was still powerful, the strengthening of its competitors meant American *relative* power had declined.

Effects of Vietnam War

Added to these systemic changes were several developments within the United States that directly damaged U.S. *absolute* power. Most profound among these were the effects of the war in Vietnam, so pervasive that the war has left its name on most of the post-1968 period. First, the war's financing disrupted the United States' remarkable economic health, damaging this foundation of national power. Second, the U.S. failure either to win the war or cut its losses severely injured American prestige worldwide, leading other nations to reassess their perceptions of American power and good judgment.

Vietnam also had dramatic psychological effects at home, reducing public support for the use of military power as an instrument of foreign policy. The result was a negative attitude in the Congress on defense spending, leading to budget cuts that cost the United States several years of military modernization even as the Soviet buildup was proceeding. Finally, and perhaps most serious, the war destroyed the consensus on containment, opening the most basic policy issues to enervating public debate.

But the domestic divisions over Vietnam were only part of the social trauma suffered by the United States in the late 1960s. They merely added to the strains on American society caused by the arrival of the children of the postwar baby boom at the age of independence (if not rebellion), and by the nation's long-delayed facing up to social injustice through the civil rights movement. Moreover, their impact was reinforced by a progressive breakdown of power in the political system: burgeoning primaries democratized the electoral process, political parties lost internal discipline and control, and the seniority system and other principles of order in Congress collapsed—just as that body was asserting its foreign policy prerogatives.

These trends continued into the early 1970s and were soon exacerbated by two further developments. The first was Nixon's Watergate scandal and the unprecedented resignation of a sitting President, which shook foreign perceptions of American stability and hurt the nation's ability to set a cohesive foreign policy. The second was the quadrupling of oil prices by the Organization of Petroleum Exporting Countries (OPEC) in 1973–74, which added to American economic difficulties, caused serious strains within U.S. alliances, and seemed to show that Third World states could use American economic dependence to coerce a change in U.S. foreign policy.

OPEC also foreshadowed another phenomenon of the 1970s: a sudden proliferation of extraordinarily complex and little understood issues—like environmental pollution, explosive population growth, rampant urbanization, worldwide food shortages, and the prospect of global-resource depletion and even catastrophic climatic change—which further threatened U.S. power and demanded unheard-of cooperation among governments. Global interdependence meant that post-Vietnam policymakers not only had to redefine old policies and find new means of executing them; they also had to fold these new issues into the policy mix and then hope the American people could digest the results.

The Impact of Public Opinion

As a cumulative result of these developments, it can be argued, the post-World War II era ended in the United States nearly two decades ago. Beginning with the Nixon Administration, American Presidents have had to deal with a much more difficult world, and to do so with relatively less power and a less-than-united people behind them. A great many of the frustrations of these last two decades can be explained as the confused efforts of the nation and its leaders to understand the new situation and fashion an appropriate policy.

Any set of broad conclusions about public opinion must be highly tentative, reflecting rough shifts in the apparent weight of opinion as revealed by incomplete and often contradictory opinion polls. Public opinion did not swing sharply or immediately as this perplexing series of events gradually unfolded. The post-Vietnam era has, however, seen significant changes in American views, with important effects on presidential elections and on U.S. foreign policy. At least four broad phases in the public mood can be discerned. (See page 12.)

The first phase, beginning in the late 1960s and continuing through the early 1970s, was dominated by the protest against American involvement in Vietnam. People not usually attentive to foreign affairs were brought strongly into the debate by their opposition to the war, and the demand for peace reinforced a general feeling that the United States should avoid foreign interventions and entanglements. Support for the use of American troops in crisis situations was the lowest in the postwar period, with one poll in 1974 even finding a plurality opposed (41 percent to 39 percent) to sending U.S. troops to meet a Soviet invasion of

Western Europe; only a third of the people felt that "defending our allies' security" was "very important." Support for defense also was at an all-time low in 1973-74. Gallup polls indicated that a plurality of from 44 to 46 percent of the people thought defense spending was too high. (See page 17.)

U.S. Suffers Successive Shocks

Toward the end of this period (and despite the negotiated withdrawal from Vietnam) the country was hit with a disheartening series of major adverse developments, including the first OPEC crisis, the onset of double-digit inflation, President Nixon's resignation and the fall of Saigon to North Vietnamese forces. This torrent of bad news did nothing to promote a speedy national recovery from the traumas of Vietnam. Bewildered, people tended to search for scapegoats, whether in the Central Intelligence Agency (CIA), the White House staff or the military. The credibility of all major institutions fell dramatically, and distrust of government became a permanent and corrosive feature of American politics. Although he never won the office in his own right, the President of phase one was Gerald R. Ford, who saw his role as restoring the integrity of government and providing "a time to heal."

After the fall of South Vietnam in April 1975, the wave of successive shocks came to a temporary halt; for a time, Americans were left alone with their thoughts. It is a fair guess that the nonattentive public left the foreign affairs arena to concentrate on domestic concerns, particularly the stagflation-ridden economy. Phase two was a period of consolidation of opinion from phase one and preparation for the major changes to come in phase three.

Throughout this period the desire for noninvolvement strengthened. Polls revealed that the majority of Americans who felt the United States should take an active role in world affairs was shrinking (from 66 percent in 1974 to 59 percent in 1978). (See page 65.) Growing preoccupation with domestic issues, downplaying of the Soviet threat and weariness with the sacrifices necessary to contain it, and a feeling of helplessness in the face of

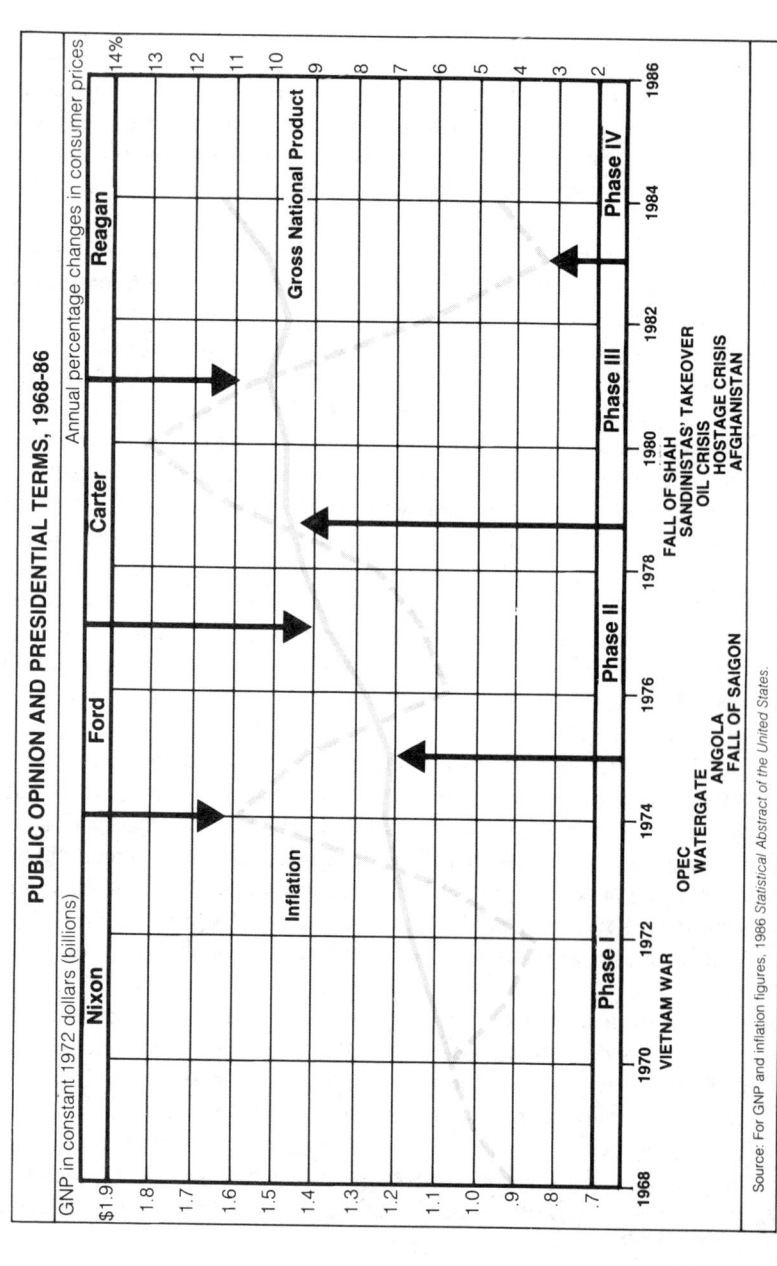

the problems of interdependence all probably contributed to apathy and inertia and to a longing for retrenchment.

But phase two was a harbinger of the future as well as an echo of the past. Although a uniform three fourths of the public still supported cooperation with the Soviet Union, Americans increasingly began to feel that the Soviets were getting the better of the bargain. *Détente* with the U.S.S.R. was attacked from the right and the word deleted from President Ford's campaign lexicon. And yet there was still no majority support for increases in defense spending; on the contrary, a strong plurality for no change in defense spending solidified. On the positive side, there was a renewed demand for values and morality in American foreign policy. In the bicentennial election of 1976, the politics of values and the democratization of the political system led to the election of a former one-term governor of Georgia, Jimmy Carter, the President of phase two.

By the winter of 1978-79, however, a third phase was beginning to emerge with unmistakable force. Polls began to reveal anxiety about a decline in American prestige, strong dissatisfaction with the reduced value of the dollar, and great concern about a growing military threat from the Soviet Union, including fear that the United States was falling behind in power and influence. Reflecting those concerns, sentiment on defense spending began to move away from a "no change" plurality toward a clear desire for growth that peaked in 1980. There was also a great increase in the number of people who felt that the U.S. commitment to the North Atlantic Treaty Organization (NATO) should be maintained or expanded, and those feeling that it was "very important" for the United States to defend its allies' security moved from a third to a half of those polled. Observing that the public's foreign policy concerns were "permeated" with self-interest, the authors of a 1978 survey for the Chicago Council on Foreign Relations found Americans both eager "to curtail commitments in certain parts of the world" and prepared to defend their interests in some "high-priority areas . . . ," "increasingly sensitive to the distinction between. . . international involvement[s]. . .that are in our self-interest and those that are not."

These trends were dramatically sharpened by events in 1979, a year (like 1968) filled with stunning developments. First, Vietnam's invasion of Cambodia (and its clear intention to dominate Laos) suggested that U.S. involvement in Vietnam might not have been the sole cause of Southeast Asia's turmoil. Then, in early 1979, came the fall of the shah of Iran followed by the second oil crisis and the return of gas lines, reminding Americans in a uniquely personal way that developments overseas could seriously affect their interests. In late summer the United States discovered an "unacceptable" Soviet brigade in Cuba which, nevertheless, it was unable to remove. Fall brought the seizure of American hostages in Tehran, and Christmas, the Soviet invasion of Afghanistan, long-running sagas which continuously reminded Americans of the seriousness of the danger abroad and the extent of American helplessness.

By the time of the 1980 presidential election, American opinion had crystallized into an assertive, even aggressive mood. People were fed up with what one analyst called "loss of control" over domestic and international events; an unprecedented 84 percent agreed that the nation was in "deep and serious trouble." After years of relative neglect, foreign affairs were once again seen as the country's most important problem. By now a majority of Americans favored a bigger military budget, agreeing that the United States was behind the U.S.S.R. in military strength. An even higher percentage felt that the CIA should step up its activities, and virtually all the tougher policy tools received the people's endorsement—including the use of trade as a diplomatic weapon, registration of young men for the draft, and the use of force in crisis situations. Public opinion experts Daniel Yankelovich and Larry Kaagan wrote in *Foreign Affairs* in 1981 that the American public had undergone "one of those decisive shifts that historians generally label as watershed events....Clearly the introspective brooding of the Ford-Carter period on the agonized question, 'Are we a good people?' can hardly contrast more sharply with today's impatient question, 'Why are we letting ourselves be pushed around?'"

The shift of public opinion from lethargic self-doubt to assertive nationalism put Ronald Reagan in the White House and provided him with a broad mandate for a strong foreign policy. Well before the 1984 election, however, people's views had shifted to some degree, and a fourth phase of the post-Vietnam era began. By late 1982 opinion polls revealed an abatement of concern about the United States falling behind the U.S.S.R. in military strength, along with a significant public consensus that the two superpowers were "about equal." According to a Chicago council survey, there was a pronounced drop in support for growth in military spending between 1978 and 1982, with a majority wanting to keep it about the same.

A Recentering of Opinion

By the 1984 election, in fact, it was becoming clear that Americans were satisfied with their country's strength but increasingly worried about peace. Apparently the President's direct language about the possibility of nuclear war, his difficulty in achieving any arms control progress with the Kremlin, and the heightened visibility of nuclear issues all caused people to have second thoughts about the Administration's extremely tough policy toward the U.S.S.R. In addition, the cold-war fear of communism's ideological appeal had yielded to a discounting of the doctrine's subversive power. According to Yankelovich and John Doble writing in *Foreign Affairs* in 1984, Americans now appeared to endorse "a relatively nonideological, pragmatic live-and-let-live attitude" toward the Soviet Union in particular, and a more accommodating and constructive approach to world affairs in general. The public wanted the country to remain strong, but for defensive rather than interventionist purposes.

There has been other evidence in the last few years that public opinion is more centrist and stable than before. People seem increasingly to be combining a renewed internationalism with self-interestedness. They remain concerned about their country's power and prestige overseas, but they also believe that foreign policy has a major impact on their prosperity through its effects on unemployment and the value of the dollar. If Americans are still as unwilling as in 1976 to have their country commit troops in areas of marginal interest, they are nevertheless as ready as in 1980 to protect clearly vital interests in Western Europe, Japan and the Middle East—if necessary with military force.

With this fourth phase, in fact, the post-Vietnam era may well have come to an end. Americans have begun to integrate the lessons of these turbulent years with those of the cold war, regaining a sense of the necessity for power without forgetting that modern conditions may limit its use. People seem increasingly to understand that the United States can exercise leadership without dominance; that internationalism is possible without intervention and activism without entrapment. Indeed, it is likely that strong elements of continuity existed throughout the post-Vietnam years, that shifts in the weight of opinion were like the swings of a car's rear wheels as it careens around corners on a snowy road, the unavoidable path of progress toward a new maturity and sophistication.

Presidents and Policy

In a democratic country like the United States, public opinion and power set the boundaries of an effective foreign policy. Public attitudes, as perceived by an Administration and reflected in people's representatives in Congress, determine the internal limits of what a President can do in foreign affairs. And power, relative to other states in the international system, sets the external bounds on the nation's ability to affect its international environment.

Furthermore, these two factors interact, sometimes beneficently, sometimes perversely. A President's success in foreign relations depends substantially upon the power at his command. But his success also has a good deal of impact on the public's support for his policies and, therefore, on its willingness to see Congress fund the policy tools needed to make U.S. power effective. Hence, foreign policy success can lead to more power in a President's hands and more successes, while foreign policy failures can reduce the power at his command and breed further disappointments. Moreover, a unified public opinion is often

VIEWS ON THE ADEQUACY OF DEFENSE SPENDING, 1969-86

Year	Too Little (percent)	About Right (percent)	Too Much (percent)
1960 (Gallup)	21	45	18
Phase I			
1969 (Gallup)	8	31	52
1971 (Gallup)	11	31	49
1973 (NORC)	11	45	38
1973 (Gallup)	13	30	46
1974 (NORC)	17	45	31
1974 (CCFR)	13	47	32
1974 (Gallup)	12	32	44
Phase II			
1975 (NORC)	17	46	31
1976 (NORC)	24	42	37
1976 (Gallup)	22	32	36
1977 (NORC)	24	45	23
1977 (Gallup)	27	40	23
1978 (NORC)	27	44	22
1978, late (CCFR)	32	45	16
Phase III			
1980 (NORC)	56	26	11
1981 (Gallup)	51	22	15
1982 (NORC)	29	36	30
1982 (Gallup)	16	31	41
1982 (CCFR)	21	52	24
Phase IV			
1983 (Gallup)	21	36	37
1985 (Gallup)	11	36	46
1986 (Gallup)	13	36	47

Sources: National Opinion Research Center (NORC), University of Chicago; Gallup and Chicago Council on Foreign Relations (CCFR) data from John E. Rielly's *American Public Opinion and U.S. Foreign Policy 1983*, (see Reading List).

critical to overseas perceptions of a nation's power and thereby can directly affect its likelihood of success in a given foreign enterprise.

A Question of Timing

What is fascinating about the recent history of American foreign policy is the way in which the relative decline of national power, shifts in public opinion and changes in presidential leadership have interacted to produce foreign policy turmoil. A major reason that recent shifts in public opinion have been so damaging is that they have usually been out of sync with the electoral process. A President elected in one phase has very often served much of his term in another, struggling all the while to adjust to rather different public attitudes. Thus, Ford, the President of phase one, was too conventional and centrist for phase two in which he served; Carter, elected in phase two, was quite unsuited for the assertiveness of phase three; and Reagan, most definitely a manifestation of phase three, has spent most of his time in power in the far more moderate climate of phase four.

To be sure, the Nixon-Ford, Carter and Reagan presidencies have not been equally vulnerable to such pressures. A lot depended on where each Administration began its official life politically, and on how clear a grasp of reality each brought to office. Broadly speaking, the Nixon-Kissinger approach now appears to have been closest to the political center of the three, a strongly pragmatic policy that lacked pronounced ideological biases. Carter and Reagan, by contrast, came into office with definite preconceived ideas—or ideologies—of the left and the right, respectively. Not surprisingly, the first Administration's centrist pragmatism enabled it to maintain its basic policy thrust even in the face of a change in chief executives, whereas both later Presidents found themselves forced to become more pragmatic, pushed by experience and public opinion toward the political center.

Still, each of these post-Vietnam Administrations fashioned a unique and identifiable approach to the conduct of foreign policy, responding in its own way to the more difficult international environment, shifts in public opinion, and the country's less dominant power. In the process Presidents Nixon, Carter and Reagan established three models that may well set the parameters for American foreign policy in the decades ahead.

2

Nixon, Kissinger and Geopolitics

In the first volume of his memoirs, Henry Kissinger laments the tendency of Americans to downplay the role of power in international relations:

> There is in America an idealistic tradition that sees foreign policy as a contest between good and evil. There is a pragmatic tradition that seeks to solve "problems" as they arise. There is a legalistic tradition that treats international issues as juridical cases. There is no geopolitical tradition.

For Kissinger and his boss, President Nixon, only the geopolitical approach made sense. Maintaining the balance of power was, in Kissinger's view, a "permanent undertaking," one that called for "not only the possession of power but the will to bring it to bear." The United States, still the strongest power but no longer predominant, would have to be ready to respond even to ambiguous and marginal challenges lest the balance tip irrevocably out of its control. Success required careful calculations of potential and actual power, a "broad view of the fabric of events," close psychological judgments, perseverance, subtlety and an ability to interrelate policies in many spheres.

Unfortunately, Kissinger felt, Americans were poorly suited to the task. Accustomed by history to finding their security in staying out of the world rather than helping to shape it, they tended to search for one-time solutions rather than steel themselves for endless involvement. Considering peace and war, diplomacy and power as two separate phases of policy, Americans tended to oscillate between crusading idealism and sullen withdrawal. They were incorrigible optimists, believing that no defeats were final and that in the end good would triumph—or, as Kissinger put it, that "American goodwill supplied its own efficacy."

Kissinger's Realism

Such breezy confidence held no place in the worldview of Kissinger, whose distinctly European cast of mind recognized the often tragic character of history and admitted the possibility that calamity might really strike this country from abroad. Kissinger's adolescence as a Jew in Nazi Germany convinced him, in a way wholly alien to the American experience, that moral rectitude was not sufficient to protect an individual or a nation from outside forces of evil. Nor were policymakers able easily to impose their will on events: "The public life of every political figure," he wrote, "is a continual struggle to rescue an element of choice from the pressure of circumstance." Statesmanship consisted of the use of power and guile against formidable odds.

By a very different route, Nixon had come to virtually the same conclusions. Former defense and energy secretary James Schlesinger once observed that Presidents tend in foreign policy to use the same techniques that have worked for them in the domestic political arena. For Nixon, power politics came naturally; the very methods that put him in the White House (and led to his forced resignation) were ideally suited to the anarchy of international relations. After leaving office, he wrote in an essay on presidential power that Presidents must "know how power operates" and "have the will to use it," appearing unpredictable, even rash, and never ruling out the use of force. Kissinger found Nixon bold and courageous in a crisis, and their conduct in office demonstrated the two officials' agreement on the importance of power in diplomacy.

It is not difficult, then, to imagine the Nixon-Kissinger reaction to the relative decline of American power. They saw it as a highly regrettable development, one carrying the possibility of grave peril for the country they served. Although well aware of the damage to American prestige caused by the Vietnam War, the two men seem to have considered the U.S. decline as inevitable, mainly stemming from systemic trends quite outside American control. Nevertheless they hoped to resist and perhaps slow the loss of U.S. predominance, to manage it in ways that would prove least damaging to U.S. interests, and (with clear understanding of the psychological nature of power) to disguise it wherever possible.

The Nixon-Kissinger Strategy

In his writings, Kissinger argues convincingly that a sophisticated strategy can go far to make up for a lack of overwhelming power. "[T]here is no escaping the need for an integrating conceptual framework," he wrote. "Good policy depends on the patient accumulation of nuances; care has to be taken that individual moves are orchestrated into a coherent strategy." Ultimately, success would turn on the strategist's ability "to create incentives or pressures in one part of the world to influence events in another."

The Nixon-Kissinger strategy for dealing with the decline of American power had four basic elements. First, Nixon and Kissinger recognized that they would have to "liquidate" the Vietnam War, the most immediate and significant drain on American power. But a great deal depended on *how* U.S. involvement in the war was ended: leaving precipitously, they believed, could have even more profound consequences for American power than the war itself. Abroad, millions of people who relied on the United States would be disheartened if the country "simply walk[ed] away from an enterprise involving two Administrations, five allied countries, and 31,000 dead as if we were switching a television channel." At home, Nixon and Kissinger feared a backlash similar to that following the "loss" of China to

Mao's Communists in 1949. The shattering of American self-confidence in a humiliating defeat could lead to extremism, despair and a "nihilistic" orgy of self-hatred that would paralyze any creative foreign policy.

With these considerations in mind, the President and his national security adviser set out to achieve a negotiated withdrawal, innocently assuming that "a tolerable outcome" would be possible in less than a year. It was a daunting task. Nixon and Kissinger believed that the men in Hanoi would settle only if Washington could create incentives for them to do so. That required continued military pressure in a "no-win" situation, the creation of a stable and militarily viable regime in a South Vietnam at war, and the maintenance of public support in the midst of increasingly violent protests at home—all to be achieved while the United States was disengaging from the conflict.

The Opening to China

The Administration hoped, of course, to increase the pressure on Hanoi through the second part of its strategy: a redressing of the balance of power to substitute for the United States' waning preponderance of power. Repeatedly, the Administration called for the creation of a pentagonal order at the top of international politics, a world in which the growing power of the People's Republic of China (PRC), Japan and a united Europe would induce a reduction of tensions between the two superpowers and provide more freedom of maneuver for all its participants. But a genuine balance of power required the downplaying of any ideological restraints on realignment and a willingness of each major power to make common cause with any other, no matter how distasteful its internal regime. Accordingly, Kissinger told the press in 1969 that the United States had "no permanent enemies and that we will judge other countries, including Communist countries...on the basis of their actions and not on the basis of their domestic ideology." Of the five powers in Kissinger's pentagonal world, the United States and Mao's China were the most distant; to create a new order, 20 years of frozen hostility between them had first to be overcome.

Even a partial rapprochement between the United States and China could put enormous additional pressure on the Soviet Union. China was the Kremlin's most immediate security concern, and the prospect of a U.S.-Chinese strategic relationship faced the Soviets with the possibility of a two-front war if they threatened the West's interests too blatantly. Geopolitics at its most audacious, the opening to China would reconfigure the balance of power containing the U.S.S.R.

Kissinger and Nixon thought that the rapprochement with China could provide several additional benefits for the United States. For Nixon, the principal gain would be in putting pressure on Hanoi to settle the Vietnam War on terms short of absolute victory. The Soviets were Vietnam's main suppliers of war matériel, and those arms and equipment had to transit China for delivery. Nixon undoubtedly saw great political benefits in the policy as well. Secure in his reputation as an anti-Communist, he could use the bold move for peace to attract support from the center and left of the political spectrum. Kissinger's approach to China was more cerebral, stemming from a confidence that giving "each Communist power a stake in better relations with us" would open new opportunities for peace. Specifically, triangular geopolitics could help lessen the Chinese threat against U.S. allies in Asia and might dampen Soviet adventurism in the Third World. Most of all, Kissinger saw it as an antidote to Vietnam-induced despair, a "breath of fresh air" proving that the United States could still be a force for good in the world.

Détente and Arms Control

Triangular geopolitics also contributed to the third element in the Nixon-Kissinger strategy: the reduction of tensions with the Soviet Union known as détente. The Administration not only hoped to end the drain on American power in Vietnam and mobilize the surrogate power of China; it also would try to lessen the major challenge with which U.S. power must deal. For Nixon and Kissinger, that threat remained the U.S.S.R., whose growing nuclear capability could destroy the United States. Putting some limits on those weapons was détente's major objective.

Détente has often been represented as a one-sided sellout to the Soviets, a willingness to pay any price in order to achieve spurious agreements that confirmed Soviet superiority and further weakened the United States. But in Kissinger's formulation, détente *included* containment. The policy combined restraints on Soviet expansion (through punishment of Moscow's adventures) with positive rewards for good behavior designed to give the Kremlin a greater stake in a peaceful and stable international order. As he later wrote in *White House Years*,

> ... we were dealing with a system too ideologically hostile for instant conciliation and militarily too powerful to destroy. We had to prevent its seizing of strategic opportunities; but we also had to have enough confidence in our own judgments to make arrangements with it that would gain time—time for the inherent stagnation of the Communist system to work its corrosion. . . .

In *Years of Upheaval*, Kissinger added:

> An American President...has a dual responsibility: He must resist Soviet expansionism. And he must be conscious of the profound risks of global confrontation. His policy must embrace both deterrence and coexistence, both containment and an effort to relax tensions. If the desire for peace turns into an avoidance of conflict at all costs, . . . peaceful nations . . . will be at the mercy of the most ruthless. Yet if we pursue the ideological conflict. . . [as] an end in itself, we will lose the cohesion of our alliances and ultimately the confidence of our people. That was what the Nixon Administration understood by détente.

The Administration's conceptual instrument for interrelating the two halves of its détente policy was linkage, the idea that, in order to obtain concrete benefits in one area of policy, the Soviet Union would have to show restraint in others. In particular, the Administration made progress in arms control and liberalization of East-West trade dependent on Soviet help in ending the Vietnam War and on the easing of tensions in Berlin and the Middle East. Measurable progress took two years and required American intransigence in more than one East-West crisis, but by

1971 the Kremlin had signed an agreement guaranteeing Western access to Berlin—thereby eliminating a historic cold-war flash point—and was seriously negotiating agreements on antiballistic missile (ABM) defense and on offensive nuclear missiles.

Although Nixon desperately wanted these negotiations to succeed, he nevertheless upheld the containment part of détente by responding brutally to a North Vietnamese offensive in May 1972: the United States undertook a major bombing campaign in the North, mined Haiphong harbor, and blockaded the North Vietnamese coastline to prevent deliveries of Soviet equipment. Although the Kremlin appears not to have put any real pressure on Hanoi, it did let the May 1972 Moscow summit and the signing of the strategic arms limitation treaty (SALT I) proceed. The first package of agreements limiting the deployment of offensive and defensive nuclear arms, these accords gave détente its most important and dramatic success.

Limiting U.S. Commitments

The fourth element of the Nixon-Kissinger strategy was, like détente, fundamentally defensive in nature. It was based on the recognition that, when resources are declining, commitments have to be scaled down. In informal remarks on Guam in July 1969 and later in his 1970 foreign policy report to the Congress, Nixon unilaterally redefined American commitments: Although the United States would continue to honor all treaty pledges and provide a nuclear shield to allies facing a nuclear threat, in the future Asian nations themselves would have to provide the manpower for their own defense.

Soon known as the Nixon Doctrine, this new definition of American commitments was more an effort to manage the decline in American power than to redress it. Under the doctrine, the Administration began to rely increasingly on influential regional states as pillars of its foreign policy. In the Middle East, Nixon put enormous confidence in the shah of Iran, even going so far as to authorize the export of virtually any military equipment the shah wanted and could pay for. In South Asia the United States supported Pakistan, and in East Asia it backed Philippine

National security adviser Henry A. Kissinger confers with President Nixon on the Paris negotiations to end the Vietnam War in November 1972.

President Ferdinand E. Marcos and South Korean President Park Chung Hee. American economic and military assistance was designed to make these states strong enough to resist Soviet pressures on their own. And when local crises seemed to risk Kremlin involvement, Nixon and Kissinger proved quite willing to threaten all-out confrontation. In the Indo-Pakistan war of 1971, and again in the October 1973 war in the Middle East, the United States went to the brink of nuclear war to protect allied states against destruction by Soviet clients.

The Strategy in Practice

Substantively, then, the Nixon Administration hoped to end the sapping of American power in Vietnam and reduce the burden of American commitments, while using détente and triangular geopolitics to blunt the Soviet threat. The elements of its strategy were mutually supporting, for the opening to China was expected to bolster détente, and détente was supposed to contribute to a settlement in Indochina. It was, in short, a realistic, sophisticated and tightly integrated approach to the world, and by the end of Nixon's first term it had achieved a certain momentum.

Though conservative in intent, the Nixon strategy was executed in bold strokes, employing secret diplomacy, dramatic gestures and at times unusual methods. The Administration's awareness of the psychological nature of power suggested a style that was bigger than life. Nixon ordered ostentatious new uniforms for the White House police, and people started talking about the "imperial presidency." Kissinger became something of a media superstar, jetting from capital to capital while engaging in secret negotiations on three continents.

Professor Bruce Mazlish has described the Nixon-Kissinger tactics as those of the white revolutionary: staging a series of dramatic acts—often measures that were advocated by the political left in the United States, like arms negotiations with the Soviets and rapprochement with China—which disarmed Nixon's critics while demonstrating American power in the service of stabilizing goals. In fact, Kissinger later admitted that it was an effort "to combine the analysis and strategy of the conservatives with the tactics of the liberals." Such maneuvers reflected a conscious decision to disguise the loss of American power under a smokescreen of razzle-dazzle diplomacy, particularly as Watergate eroded the strength of the presidency at home and the United States abroad. The attempt to compensate for the decline in American power "imposed a style of diplomacy leaning toward the spectacular; a show of driving self-assurance. . . . We needed a visible, if necessary [a] theatrical, affirmation that America would survive its anguish and still build a better world."

White House Control

Undertaking such a daring policy in a time when national consensus was disintegrating meant, in effect, that the White House had to substitute its will for that of the nation. Nixon's and Kissinger's reaction to the post-Vietnam collapse of foreign policy consensus was simply to ignore it, to keep the bureaucracy and the

Congress largely in the dark and assume that the national interest need only be determined by geopolitical reasoning from the top down, not through the democratic process from the bottom up. Policymaking was centralized in the White House, using techniques that were highly personalized, secretive and authoritarian, even conspiratorial. The departments were tasked to do "hypothetical" or "planning" studies of matters that were actually the subject of ongoing negotiations directed by the White House, allowing Kissinger to "use the bureaucracy without revealing our purposes." As national security adviser he set up a "back channel" for direct communication with Moscow through Soviet Ambassador Anatoly F. Dobrynin and used it to achieve breakthroughs in sensitive negotiations. Often the official U.S. negotiators did not know what was going on, nor was Secretary of State William P. Rogers or the American ambassador in Moscow informed. Such practices fitted well with the character of the President they served, for Kissinger found Nixon paranoid about his political enemies, notoriously distrustful of the bureaucracy, fearful of leaks, and temperamentally unable to deal with subordinates on difficult subjects.

The Failure of Détente

Although Kissinger admits that these methods caused a variety of embarrassing difficulties and were hardly models for government organization, he also points out that they produced "the SALT breakthrough, the opening to China, a Berlin agreement, the Peking and the Moscow summits without any setback." Certainly one could argue persuasively that some degree of centralization and secrecy was essential to the Administration's considerable successes: it is hard to imagine that the opening to China or the SALT I accords could have been accomplished in public view or without direct White House control. But such methods could not survive the crippling impact of Watergate, and it is difficult to believe that their ademocratic character could have prospered for long in the American context—however useful they may have seemed in a time of domestic turmoil.

It was not long before détente came under attack. The left

complained that the Administration had not achieved what, in fact, it had never expected: a complete reconciliation with the U.S.S.R. and the liberalization of the Soviet domestic system. As Kissinger said of détente, "we had conceived it as managing the relations among adversaries; our critics faulted it for falling short of establishing friendship." Those on the right argued, as they do today, that no agreement with Moscow could possibly be beneficial to the United States: "They equated negotiations with Moscow with the moral disarmament of America." Many in Congress and the public also became disillusioned with the seeming amorality of the balance of power: the willingness to deal with any nation, the rapprochement with Communist governments in the Soviet Union and China, and the supporting of authoritarian regimes in the Third World.

As criticism mounted, Kissinger, by then secretary of state, found it more and more difficult to secure the support he needed for successful diplomacy. Defense spending was scrutinized and cut following the U.S. withdrawal from Vietnam. Congress linked "most-favored-nation" trade status for the Soviets to Moscow's liberalization of Jewish emigration and insisted on "equal aggregates" in the next round of SALT negotiations, tying diplomacy to goals Kissinger thought infeasible or undesirable. Congress even cut off covert aid to elements the United States was supporting in the Angolan civil war, leading to failure there of the containment part of détente.

In the end, the Nixon-Kissinger strategy achieved only partial success. In his zeal to negotiate with the Soviets and the Chinese, Kissinger neglected and even antagonized America's traditional allies. His "Year of Europe" in 1973 became a year of bickering and Watergate, and Japan was deeply shocked by the Administration's failure to provide advance consultations on the U.S. reconciliation with China. In his concern for the global balance of power, Kissinger treated nearly all regional or local disputes as East-West problems, with two unfortunate results. First, Third World areas not considered important to global geopolitics were virtually ignored, and the Administration gave short shrift to the entire range of new interdependence issues. Second, in those areas which *were* deemed vital in the East-West struggle, almost any crisis could seem of transcendent importance to the balance of power, thereby justifying the use of virtually any policy tool or even a confrontation with the Soviets.

As the Nixon years merged into the Ford interregnum (1974-77), the strategy of controlled retreat and negotiated détente seemed to falter. Although the Administration succeeded in at last departing Vietnam, the settlement took not one year but four and cost another 20,000 American lives. Moreover, opposition to the war proved so potent that the Congress refused to approve more U.S. aid to the South when the North launched its final offensive in 1975. With the fall of Saigon, Asian leaders had to accommodate to a weakened American role in an altered balance of power. Thailand asked the American military to leave its soil, and the Philippines temporarily turned down a billion dollar bases renewal offer. At the same time, détente was not deterring Soviet/Cuban adventurism in Africa and elsewhere, and SALT I seemed powerless to prevent a massive Soviet weapons buildup. Congress, hopelessly fragmented and congenitally unable to provide leadership itself, had earlier enacted legislation limiting the use of executive agreements that bypassed the Senate's advice and consent and restricting the power of the President to use military force abroad. Such legislation codified the new, Watergate-induced weakness of the executive branch.

A Sophisticated Strategy

For all its shortcomings, however, the Nixon-Kissinger strategy left a powerful legacy. Although the Administration failed to sustain public support and in the end destroyed its *internal* freedom of maneuver, it went very far in addressing the *external* problem of American power. Its opening to China fundamentally transformed the structure of world politics and provided all future Administrations with new flexibility and a powerful anti-Soviet tool. The Administration's arms control agreements, however inadequate, began a process which no future President could long ignore. Even détente, with all its setbacks, provided a model of lessened ideological hostility that has found a powerful popular echo in the American people's more pragmatic attitude toward relations with the Soviet Union.

But the most important legacy of the Nixon-Kissinger policy lies in the intellectual premises on which they approached the post-Vietnam world. Here was an intelligent, conceptual, yet pragmatic policy that avoided simplistic or ideologically slanted formulations, that began with realistic background assumptions about the world and how it worked, that held a clear-eyed assessment of the national interest and the resources available to support it and devised a sophisticated strategy to serve its objectives. Perhaps most impressive, while not downplaying the seriousness of the Soviet threat, Nixon's policy simultaneously recognized and addressed both the need to contain the Soviet Union and the need to live with it, the imperatives of national security and of nuclear survival. In this blend of the seemingly contradictory, this mixture of cold war and conciliation, Nixon and Kissinger prefigured the framework of a mature American foreign policy.

3

Jimmy Carter, Denial of Power and the Quest for Values

The quintessential post-Vietnam President, Jimmy Carter arrived at the White House with remarkably little experience in foreign affairs. Carter, who had never held national office, made a virtue of his inexperience, campaigning against the Washington establishment that had brought the country Vietnam and Watergate. The new President was a quick study and worked hard to educate himself on international affairs. But it is unlikely that his convictions about foreign policy were deeply rooted, or that he had a vast store of the "intellectual capital" which, Kissinger warned, "was consumed, not created, by high office."

The former Georgia governor's approach to foreign policy was very different from that of his Republican predecessors. A born-again Christian, Carter felt that the country needed a period of "national repentance," and he wanted to restore basic American values to the nation's foreign policy. The new President was also impatient with the traditional caution and incrementalism of diplomacy. Where Kissinger had held that a "statesman's test is not only the exaltation of his goals but the catastrophe he averts," Carter adopted an audacious, high-risk strategy, pushing for immediate gains on many fronts. An engineer by training, he approached policy analysis in a highly rational and mechanistic way, investing gargantuan effort in mastering the technical detail of complex international issues but without any overarching or unifying concept. Close associates found his thought processes linear and disaggregated, tending to list items and events without a sense of their mutual causality and interrelationships, in contrast to Kissinger's conceptual and integrating approach.

A Different Sense of Power

Despite these differences, Carter agreed with Nixon and Kissinger that the relative decline in American power was ongoing and irreversible. He warned Americans in his Inaugural Address "that 'more' is not necessarily 'better,' that even our great nation has its recognized limits, and that we can neither answer all questions nor solve all problems." In fact, Carter considered the idea of limits "the subliminal theme" of his presidency, whether expressed in terms of energy supplies and natural resources, or the Federal government's capacity to provide a "bottomless cornucopia" for the people, or the nation's ability "to influence others or to control international events."

But unlike Nixon or Kissinger, Carter did not seem to feel that this state of affairs was entirely bad. Indeed, the Administration initially acted as if it believed that too much American power overseas would inevitably produce Vietnams and too much presidential power within the domestic political system would spawn more Watergates. So where Nixon and Kissinger worked to slow and manage the decline in American power, the Carter Administration at first took a number of actions that had the effect of accelerating the decline. And where his Republican predecessors tried to make the United States look bigger than life, Carter set out to demythologize the presidency and reduce American commitments abroad, as well as the means to carry them out.

Carter seems to have lacked an intuitive feel for power, what Kissinger identified in Nixon as "an extraordinary instinct for the jugular." The new President's political upbringing had been remarkably different from the Californian's; he seemed almost to believe that the powers of the presidency were due more to the formality of having won the election than to the political skill with which a President operates after arriving at the White House. On Inauguration Day Carter walked down Pennsylvania Avenue as a "tangible indication of some reduction in the imperial status of the President," and he took further steps (like banning the traditional "Ruffles and Flourishes" at public appearances and carrying his own luggage when traveling) to "convince the people that barriers between them and top officials in Washington were being broken down." Instead, it is likely that such self-effacement convinced his political opponents (and even many in his own party) that he was not a President they needed to take seriously.

Carter showed a similar inattention to the psychological nature of power in foreign relations. In his Inaugural Address, he said that American strength should be "based not merely on the size of an arsenal but on the nobility of ideas," a concept which he implemented in a variety of early decisions that downplayed military power. Having campaigned on a 5 percent cut in the defense budget, the new President decided to withdraw troops from South Korea, to cancel the B-1 bomber, and to defer production of the neutron bomb—each decision apparently made without an appreciation of the cumulative signals being sent about American power and the President's willingness to use it. Again, the likely result was that neither allies nor adversaries felt they had to take American power seriously.

New Threats to the National Interest

These actions were based on a very different set of assumptions about the nature of the international system, as well as on a changed assessment of likely challenges to the national interest. In his memoirs, Secretary of State Cyrus R. Vance argued that the Nixon-Kissinger policy was "too narrowly rooted in the concept of an overarching U.S.-Soviet 'geopolitical' struggle." Vance believed that "the bipolar focus of the postwar period [had] given way to a more complicated set of relationships in which power was more diffuse." As he put it, "the polarized world of the 1950s, already giving way to diversity and the diffusion of power in the 1960s, became the interdependent, multipolar world of the 1970s." In such a world, the Soviet threat had to take its place among other policy concerns.

In fact, where Nixon and Kissinger attempted a sophisticated effort to deal with the Soviet threat, Carter at first downplayed its importance and urgency. The U.S.S.R. was viewed as a gerontocracy whose leaders knew the horrors of war firsthand. Managed by a calcified bureaucracy, it was seen as a conservative, status quo power with a lot to lose if it disrupted international peace and stability. Of course, the United States had to maintain enough military power to deter a Soviet nuclear attack, and Carter acted to modernize the U.S. strategic nuclear arsenal with 200 MX missiles (despite their basing problems) and to shore up the NATO alliance (with new medium-range nuclear weapons). But with the considerable exception of national security adviser Zbigniew Brzezinski, Administration officials did not see the Kremlin as a clear and present danger to American survival.

From this perspective, the Carter Administration denounced Kissinger's "excessive preoccupation with practicing balance-of-power politics" and his tendency to view every Third World nation as a pawn in the East-West struggle. In contrast to that "globalist" stance, the Administration deliberately adopted a more "regionalist" posture in Third World crises, contending that their origins lay in indigenous economic, social and political conditions, and that the best way to handle Soviet expansionism was to deal with Third World problems on their merits. Even should Moscow temporarily extend its influence over one or another country, the United States could relax in the confidence that Soviet imperialism had natural limits. As events in Egypt demonstrated, Moscow's successes in the Third World were not always permanent.

Moreover, Carter and Vance believed that the United States had to be careful about getting involved. There were limits to what it could accomplish in complex Third World situations; Vietnam showed what small interventions might lead to. Following such logic, the President failed to dispatch American forces when Zaire's Shaba province was twice invaded from Angolan territory; he refused to send a carrier task force into waters off Somalia to counter obvious Soviet support of Ethiopia in the Ogaden war of 1977–79; and the Administration kept its options open in Thailand when the Southeast Asia Treaty Organization (SEATO) disbanded, saying that in a crisis the United States "would make its own judgment depending on the specific circumstances."

For the Carter Administration, the military threat to American survival was surpassed by the problematic, complex and insidious impact of global interdependence on American economic welfare and perhaps on planetary survival. Carter's economic philosophy was premised on the idea that America's welfare was directly tied to economic and political conditions overseas. It recognized that Third World nations increasingly supplied raw materials for American industry and markets for American goods. In Secretary Vance's view, American interdependence with the Third World made it important that the United States understand "the changes taking place in global political, economic, and social conditions" so that it could "address a wide range of problems that affected the well-being and development of Third World nations."

The Carter Administration's strategy for dealing with these challenges to the national interest involved three interrelated elements. First, the United States would be more accommodating to Third World demands for a bigger slice of the planet's economic resources and a greater role in the international political and economic system. Rather than building military power to out-confront the Kremlin in the Third World, the Administration would out-compete it there in supporting national development and addressing basic human needs, capitalizing on American economic and technological strengths. Carter appointed Andrew Young, a black civil rights activist, as U.S. ambassador to the UN, partly to provide a visible indication of a new American attitude and forthcomingness to Third World concerns.

Second, the Administration felt it was very important to defuse ongoing Third World conflicts, especially where traditional U.S. policies had fostered anti-American hostility and charges of imperialism. Impelled by his Christian commitment and recognizing that America's prestige was dependent on more than its power, Carter hoped to make major progress on the Arab-Israeli dispute, to place the United States firmly on the majority side of the great black-white division in Africa, and to show in the Panama Canal settlement that the United States was willing to respect Third World sovereignty even in a matter important to its own national security.

Here President Carter took enormous political risks and scored major achievements. The Panama treaties were approved in spite of a bruising and politically costly fight in Congress; the United States cooperated with the British in achieving majority rule in Zimbabwe; and, most impressively, the President twice committed his personal prestige to a Middle East settlement, first in the Camp David talks and then in an unprecedented regional mediation effort to secure the Egyptian-Israeli Peace Treaty. No President with a sensible concern for his own and the nation's power would have taken such gambles for peace. And yet it was just such political insensitivity, combined with Carter's preoccupation with detail, that brought him successes—along with his presidency's ultimate failure.

Third, the Carter Administration eventually hoped "to weave a worldwide web" of bilateral political and economic relations with what Brzezinski called "emerging regional 'influentials,' " countries like Venezuela, Brazil, Nigeria, Saudi Arabia, Iran, India and Indonesia. Rather than concentrate on providing military aid to Third World allies, as in the Nixon Doctrine, the Carter Administration hoped to begin forging multifaceted, in-depth relationships that would at once recognize and reinforce the new multipolar shape of world politics. To illustrate this Third World focus, the President traveled much more frequently to less-industrialized countries than his predecessors, becoming the first chief executive ever to visit sub-Saharan Africa.

The Quest for Values

Taken together, these measures constituted a shift from geopolitics to "world-order politics," readying the nation to deal with the real challenges of a multipolar international system. But the

President Carter with national security adviser Zbigniew Brzezinski (center) and Secretary of State Cyrus Vance at Camp David, Maryland, in 1977.

Carter Administration's intended move away from the East-West competition to Third World and global issues reflected more than just a different sense of the dangers the country faced. Carter wanted to make the U.S. stance in the world more "humane and moral." By rediscovering what it was for in the world instead of remaining principally preoccupied with what it opposed, the United States would realign its policies with the trend of historical forces, perhaps compensating for reduced might by increased right.

As it turned out, part of the effort to restore traditional values to American foreign policy pointed in the same practical directions as Nixon's supposedly amoral approach. The 1979 recognition of China and Carter's Middle East diplomacy both built on foundations laid by his predecessors. Overall, however, Carter's concept of morality was fundamentally contrary to the whole Nixon-Kissinger way of doing business. Where balance-of-power politics required the United States to align itself with any nation, no matter how repressive or authoritarian, which could help maintain the balance against the Soviet Union, Carter told an audience in 1977 at Notre Dame University that "Being confident of our own future, we are now free of that inordinate fear of communism which once led us to embrace any dictator who joined us in that fear." Nor would the Administration resort to methods less noble than its purposes:

> We are confident that the democratic methods are the most effective, and so we are not tempted to employ improper tactics here at home or abroad. . . .For too many years, we've been willing to adopt the flawed and erroneous principles and tactics of our adversaries, sometimes abandoning our own values for theirs. . . .This approach failed, with Vietnam the best example of its intellectual and moral poverty.

Could a nation concerned about the limits of power afford simultaneously to shape, as Brzezinski put it, both "a world more congenial to our values *and* [italics added] more compatible with our interests"? Having watched the great practical benefits that desegregation brought to the American South, Carter thought both were possible and denied that the nation had to choose between the ideal and the practical. On the contrary, he wrote, "Our country has been strongest and most effective when morality and commitment to freedom and democracy have been most clearly emphasized in our foreign policy."

Human Rights Stance

Impelled by his own religious convictions and led by a Congress fresh from its struggles with Kissinger, Carter began to speak out on human rights violations, not only in the Soviet Union (where he sent a highly publicized letter to dissident Andrei D. Sakharov), but also in friendly or allied countries like Brazil, Argentina, Chile, Somoza's Nicaragua, South Korea, the Philippines, Thailand and Indonesia. When exhortation failed, tougher measures were added, like suspending arms shipments and security assistance to violators and voting against loans to them by international financial institutions. Within a few months, Carter sensed that the human rights campaign had ignited a spark among the press and the public as "the central theme of our foreign policy," and he professed "no inclination to douse the growing flames."

The President also took a strong moral stand with regard to the militarization of the international system, making nuclear nonproliferation, superpower arms control, and reductions in conventional arms sales all priorities in his foreign policy. It was "always obvious," he wrote, that both the United States and the U.S.S.R. had "far more weapons than would ever be needed..."; the "unbelievable destruction" they represented weighed constantly on his mind. Of course, Nixon and Kissinger had recognized the dangers of the strategic nuclear competition and worked to defuse it; but they were also aware that the Soviets were tough negotiating partners, that nonproliferation efforts could alienate allies and cost American companies billions in nuclear energy sales abroad, and that conventional arms sales were critical to the success of the Nixon Doctrine and lubricated all sorts of diplomatic transactions.

No such countervailing concerns inhibited the Carter Administration. For example, where Kissinger had spent four years maneuvering the Soviets into SALT I, Carter rejected Secretary Vance's preference for consolidating the modest limits negotiated by Ford at Vladivostok and instead sent him to Moscow—just two months after the Administration took office—with an offer of a 20 to 25 percent cut in offensive forces. Carter also sponsored the Nuclear Nonproliferation Act of 1978, prohibiting nuclear exports to any country not accepting full international safeguards; and the Administration took strong public action against suspected proliferators, cutting off aid to Pakistan and strenuously opposing reactor sales by France and West Germany to various developing countries. Finally, believing that growing stockpiles of ever more sophisticated conventional arms were likely to increase the destructiveness of Third World conflicts while absorbing resources desperately needed for development, the President set a dollar limit on U.S. arms sales to the Third World and determined to use arms transfers only as an exceptional instrument of foreign policy. Carter also sought to restrain American arms makers from developing weapons solely for export, and he engaged both the U.S.S.R. and American allies in discussions on jointly reducing the annual level of all industrialized states' arms sales to the Third World.

The President's effort to restore values to American foreign policy was not, however, restricted to policy substance. In his campaign, Carter condemned the "Lone Ranger" style of Brzezinski's predecessor and was critical of how the Nixon Administration had developed policy "out of sight of the American public and without the participation of Congress." The Georgian promised, if elected, an open, honest and responsive government, saying he would never lie to the American people. As he put it at Notre Dame:

> ...we are confident of the good sense of American people, and so we let them share in the process of making foreign policy decisions. We can thus speak with the voices of 215 million, and not just of an isolated handful.

The President's openness and sincerity sometimes led to political embarrassment, as when he revealed after the invasion of Afghanistan that he had fundamentally changed his view of the Soviets, or when he publicly lamented America's national malaise. More importantly, where Nixon and Kissinger had imposed their own policy conception on the nation, Carter's open Administration brought post-Vietnam dissension right inside, filling many political jobs with mildly left-of-center policy analysts who had achieved prominence by opposing the Vietnam War.

At the highest levels, in fact, Carter brought in men as dissimilar in their views as Vance, Brzezinski, Young and Harold Brown, making them relatively coequal and promising a team effort. Unfortunately, these officials differed on the most fundamental elements of policy, as the all-too-public struggle between Vance and Brzezinski revealed. Vance, a lawyer by profession, was so eager to moderate U.S.-Soviet tensions and so determined to negotiate differences that he despaired when the Soviet invasion of Afghanistan destroyed the "balance" between conciliation and toughness in U.S. policy toward Moscow and resigned when the President turned from the frustrations of negotiating with the chaotic Iranian government to a military rescue mission. Brzezinski, on the other hand, was so anti-Soviet and so insistent on the forceful upholding of American interests that he repeatedly rubbed U.S. recognition of China in the Kremlin's face and wondered whether the Administration might not have "lost" Iran because it hesitated to endorse a military coup there. Though each man brought special strengths to the Administration, Carter's own lack of a comprehensive worldview left him incapable of disciplining their wide policy differences. The result was an Administration at war with itself, a lack of strategy at the highest levels of policy and hesitation and inconsistency in American diplomacy.

The Frustrations of a Post-Vietnam Policy

Taken as a whole, the record of the Carter Administration represents something of a paradox in recent American foreign policy. Undoubtedly, the Administration did a great deal to highlight American values in the U.S. approach to the world, and it showed uncommon courage in tackling the difficult political problems and interdependence issues which increasingly crowd the agenda of world politics. Moreover, its effectiveness as a negotiator and conciliator led to an impressive variety of concrete achievements, like the Panama Canal treaties, normalization of relations with China, the Camp David accords and the Egyptian-Israeli Peace Treaty, the NATO nuclear modernization agreement and the SALT II treaty. And yet the Carter Administration is remembered by most Americans for the fall of the shah, the takeover by the Sandinistas in Nicaragua, the second oil crisis, the Soviet invasion of Afghanistan, and especially the Iranian hostage crisis. In 1980, it was defeated at the polls after one term in office.

Much of the Carter Administration's trouble resulted from a lack of policy coherence and the divided counsels of its top officials. Carter was also caught by the dramatic shift between phases two and three of post-Vietnam public opinion, forcing on him the unenviable choice between stubborn persistence in an unpopular course or abandoning his declared principles in a belated effort to adapt. Moreover, having proclaimed policies like human rights so loudly in terms of high principle, the Administration stood open to charges of hypocrisy and backtracking when it made sensible accommodations with reality.

Disappointments Mount

Other failures grew out of the Administration's very ambition. Eager and impatient, it took on an awesome array of extraordinarily difficult tasks, in the end seriously overloading its own decisionmaking circuits. According to Brzezinski, a setback as serious as the fall of the shah simply overtook the Carter White House as it wrestled simultaneously with critical turning points in the Camp David process, SALT II, China recognition and the crisis in Nicaragua. Decisionmakers also seemed not to anticipate that the Administration's lofty goals might collide when applied in the real world. For example, the effort to support the nonproliferation objective by obstructing a multibillion dollar nuclear technology sale to Brazil seriously compromised U.S. relations with that "regional influential," while the vigorous human rights offensive alienated other Third World leaders.

In fact, the Carter Administration appears not to have thought many of its policies through carefully enough to ensure smooth execution or to distinguish between the desirable and the possible. In his memoirs, Carter admits that he "did not fully grasp all the ramifications" of his human rights policy, and he was shocked when the Kremlin, still smarting from his public support of Sakharov, rejected Vance's initial arms control proposals out of hand. Though his nonproliferation policy raised global awareness of the problem and may have somewhat slowed the spread of nuclear weapons, Carter found he had insufficient leverage over prospective proliferators, who could get the technology elsewhere. Efforts to restrict conventional arms sales, too, proved disappointing. The arms-transfer talks with the Soviets broke down; sales by major NATO allies jumped 78 percent during Carter's term in office (even U.S. deliveries increased 14 percent); and, because of the importance of supplying U.S. arms to support the Egyptian-

Israeli Peace Treaty, the campaign for restraint was formally abandoned in 1980.

Beyond these practical problems, the Carter Administration's basic worldview seems to have been at best ahead of its time, at worst simply mistaken. Though obviously of great potential importance, economic and global issues were too diffuse, distant and uncertain to provide the basis for either a coherent policy or a new consensus in the domestic body politic. Attention to morality in foreign policy was indeed a popular demand, but not one to be pursued at the expense of more-vital national interests. With regard to the importance of the Third World, too, Carter got the trend right, but he was too far ahead of the national consciousness.

Most serious, though, was the President's effort to move relations with the Soviet Union from center stage. Carter was right to argue that Americans should free themselves from the kind of all-encompassing fear of communism that led them into Vietnam, right to argue that the United States ought not to worry so much about Moscow that it failed to address Third World problems on their merits or compromised American values in desperate efforts to build anti-Soviet coalitions. But the Soviet threat was real and growing in the late 1970s, and ironically it became most obvious precisely in those Third World conflicts and regional problems that Carter hoped to detach from the East-West struggle.

Events ultimately demonstrated these failures of policy and analysis. The President who had wanted to make real cuts in strategic arms had to suspend efforts to obtain Senate ratification of the SALT II treaty and concentrate on responding to the Soviet invasion of Afghanistan. The President who wished above all to avoid entrapping his country in another Vietnam became ensnared in the effort to obtain the release of American hostages in Tehran, with devastating effects on his presidency. The President who distrusted military power and emphasized U.S. economic and technological strengths wound up recommending increases in the defense budget and committing his country (in the Carter Doctrine) to repel with force any outside attempt to gain control of the Persian Gulf. Most poignantly, the President who had come to Washington determined to restore trust between government and its people left office doubting the spiritual health of the people he served.

Long-term Contributions

Carter's frustrations should not, however, obscure the lasting value of much in his approach to American foreign relations. The President performed a valuable service in reminding the country that the Soviet challenge might best be met by dealing with the Third World conditions on which it thrives, by indirect and largely nonmilitary means. He was right to reject Kissinger's notion that the pro-U.S. alignment of any state, no matter how insignificant, was vital to American interests. His effort thus to restrict what American strategist Bernard Brodie called "the outer limits of the truly vital" rested on another piece of real wisdom: that commitments must be kept in line with available resources, ends measured against means. In these ways, Carter's was a mature policy that reflected the new conditions of world politics and American power.

President Carter should also be remembered positively for his explicit broadening of the agenda of American foreign policy. The global issues, economic concerns and Third World problems that so concerned him will surely have increasingly serious impacts on the nation's security and welfare. If Carter was ahead of his time in seeking a multipolar world where power is diffused and deployed in other than military forms, future policymakers should at least credit him for not being mired in a militaristic approach that served to perpetuate a bipolar, cold-war world.

Finally, few would question the importance of values in American foreign relations, however unrealistic Carter's assumptions about the costs involved in their unqualified pursuit. Americans do want their country to stand for something, to be right and do good in the world, even though they also want their foreign policy to defend effectively their own self-interests. And certainly the people want to be listened to in the decisionmaking process: throughout the post-Vietnam era, an average of nearly 60 percent of them have wanted public opinion to be more influential in making foreign policy. Though the people will not tolerate an Administration that does not know its own mind, they expect policymakers to respond to democratic pressure. Finding the proper balance between doing right and doing well, creating a policy which is both internally coherent and reflective of public opinion—herein lies much of the challenge to future American foreign relations.

4

Reagan and the Restoration of American Power

In the midst of his 1980 campaign for the presidency, Ronald Reagan told Bill Moyers that he knew he was going to win "for one simple reason. . . . the American people want somebody in command." That remark captured in a single phrase the preoccupation with national power that is key to the Reagan foreign policy.

Like all his post-Vietnam predecessors, Reagan understands that the United States has suffered relative decline as a world power over the past 15 to 20 years. But unlike Nixon or Carter, this President contends that the American decline can be reversed, that the country can be restored to something like the predominance it enjoyed in the decade or two following World War II. The reason is not only Reagan's innate optimism, which itself contrasts with the rather pessimistic outlooks of Carter, Nixon and Kissinger. It is also that he considers the decline to have been the result not of broad, systemic forces beyond the nation's control but rather of American failures that can be corrected. Indeed, if there is any one force that has driven the Reagan foreign policy, it is dismay with the decline of American power under Carter and a determination to bring America back.

Rebuilding National Power

Not surprisingly, then, President Reagan made rebuilding the concrete elements of American power the foundation of his foreign policy. Economic recovery —restoring the nation's base of potential foreign policy strength—was his clear priority during his first year in office, and his success in ramming a major economic program through Congress led many observers to reconsider their conclusions about the weakness of the presidency in the post-Watergate era. The Administration also made a determined effort to strengthen and expand U.S. alliances and security relationships in order to better aggregate the power of the free world. And the President has consistently supported the biggest peacetime rearmament program in American history, aiming to rebuild U.S. military power after a decade of post-Vietnam neglect.

In fact, Reagan has restored military power to a central position among the tools of American statecraft. Where Carter seemed to deny its relevance in most situations and Kissinger considered it a useful adjunct to diplomacy in some situations, Reagan seems to feel that military power ought to be directly applicable in nearly every situation. Thus, not only did he use the U.S. military in Grenada to rescue American citizens and snuff out Cuban expansion; he also put the Marines into extraordinarily difficult circumstances in Beirut, Lebanon, only to withdraw them after they had suffered severe casualties. Most obvious, of course, has been Reagan's continuous military pressure on the Sandinista rulers of Nicaragua and his escalating retaliation against Libya, culminating in the April 1986 bombing of Tripoli and Benghazi.

In addition to its preference for military power, the Reagan Administration has used all the "harder," more aggressive instruments of foreign policy far more extensively and boldly than any of its recent predecessors. Whereas the Carter Administration concentrated U.S. foreign aid to the Third World on economic objectives, Reagan has refocused the program on security. From 1980 to 1986, U.S. economic assistance (bilateral and multilateral) declined 8 percent while security assistance rose 130 percent; grants of military equipment to U.S. allies rose by some 600 percent. Under the Reagan Doctrine, the Administration has openly campaigned for covert assistance to armed insurgencies fighting against Soviet-backed regimes in Afghanistan, Nicaragua, Cambodia and Angola. Most strikingly, the revelation of activities like the 1984 mining of Nicaraguan harbors and the covert sale of weapons to Iran at a time when the United States was openly working for a prohibition on such sales indicate that Reagan is also willing to employ what Carter stigmatized as "improper tactics" overseas.

Images of Power

This attention to the American economy and the preference for military and other hard policy tools also indicate that Reagan, unlike his immediate predecessor, understands the psychological nature of power. In fact, he seems to know intuitively that a nation's power depends on other statesmen's perceptions, not only of its actual power, but also of its leaders' willingness to use it. Accordingly, the new President quickly did a number of things to send signals of his toughness, from firing unionized air traffic controllers after an illegal strike to shooting down two Libyan warplanes in the Gulf of Sidra. A man who knows how to use the media for effect, Reagan set aside Carter's tendency to tell the American people everything in favor of a calculated effort to show determination and resolve. Hence, he spoke out dramatically about the Soviet "evil empire" and even about how nuclear weapons might be used in a crisis. The Reagan Administration also likes to speak with actions: its fondness for using military power for demonstration purposes led it to recommission several World War II battleships which can show the flag (and their 16-inch guns) with helpful political effects.

Equally important to Reagan's efforts to project images of power has been the way in which his domestic political successes—culminating in his overwhelming reelection in 1984—gave him a reputation as a skilled leader, a man who knows what he wants and how to get it. Even his personal attributes—his horseback-riding, sagebrush-clearing, wood-chopping persona, with the "right stuff" to take a bullet in the chest and still oppose gun control—all projected the image of a President and a country unwilling to be pushed around. Yet in spite of being toughminded and stubborn, Reagan has been quite willing to compromise, to take "70 or 80 percent of what it is I'm trying to get . . . and then continue to try to get the rest in the future." He is even magnanimous toward his political enemies, a disarming trait that seems to reinforce the sense of his personal command.

Unfortunately, these psychological aspects of power are particularly vulnerable to adverse developments not always in the chief executive's control. Health problems, the loss of Republican control of the Senate in spite of vigorous White House campaigning, the mismanaged and inconclusive discussions with Soviet leader Mikhail S. Gorbachev at Reykjavik, Iceland, and the President's failure to control the operations of the National Security Council (NSC) staff on Iran and aid to Nicaragua's anti-Sandinista rebels, known as contras, seriously damaged the image of a President in command during the latter months of 1986. As the political climate grows colder and as the Senate's loss makes its impact felt in fewer White House political victories, the image of national power which Reagan had so personified is also suffering, and his underlying policies are becoming more apparent.

Return to the Cold War

From that perspective, it may be unfortunate that the Reagan Administration's extreme emphasis on the restoration of American power and prestige has sometimes seemed virtually an end in itself. Gone is the daunting array of specific goals set out by the Carter Administration, the intricate geopolitical strategy of the Nixon years. In their place, Reagan brings an overriding personal intuition and a set of fixed beliefs about world politics and his country's future.

In contrast to Jimmy Carter, who bore the presidency with great anguish and never found a consistent sense of direction, Ronald Reagan told one interviewer that he never stays up nights worrying about decisions because he came to settled conclusions on most things long ago. Close observers believe this President thinks anecdotally (rather than analytically like Nixon and Kissinger or serially like Carter), relying on instincts that have often proved more accurate than his advisers' reasoned forecasts but sometimes lead him dangerously astray. Showing little of the detailed knowledge of international issues that distinguished Carter among recent Presidents, Reagan draws from his own secure sense of identity the courage to act decisively on his beliefs, whether invading Grenada, pulling forces out of Lebanon, bombing Libyan targets or making vast changes in the national economy.

In place of Kissinger's sophisticated conception of international politics, Reagan's global vision is stark and without ambiguity. His worldview is a throwback to the 1950s, the period when he first became politically active and the height of the cold war. In contrast to the multipolar view of the Carter Administration and the pentagonal world order favored by Kissinger, Reagan sees the world as unredeemably bipolar and the Soviet Union as the overriding, direct threat to American interests. The fact that Soviet power is overwhelmingly military in form means to Reagan that the danger is ultimately to this country's physical survival and the preservation of its cherished liberties, again in contrast to Carter's focus on threats to American economic well-being. And the military nature of the Soviet threat also justifies the Reagan affinity for military power as the major instrument of U.S. foreign policy.

Reagan has, in fact, gone much further than Nixon and Kissinger in holding Moscow responsible for virtually every challenge to U.S. interests worldwide, from Central America to the Middle East. Operating through a group of proxy states like Cuba, Vietnam and Libya and "willing to commit any crime, to lie, to cheat" and to support international terrorism, the Kremlin is viewed as a revolutionary government, driven by Communist

Terry Arthur, The White House

President Reagan confers with advisers (l. to r.) Secretary of Defense Caspar Weinberger, Vice President George Bush, Secretary of State George Shultz, then CIA Director William Casey and then White House Chief of Staff Donald Regan.

ideology to seek world domination—a view radically different from the status quo power envisioned during most of the Carter years. Working from that perspective, the initial Reagan objective in the Middle East was to bypass the Arab-Israeli dispute and forge a "strategic consensus" against the Soviets; in Central America the aim is to stop the Sandinistas from making Nicaragua into "another Cuba"; and in southern Africa the Administration has predicated Namibia's independence on withdrawal of Cuban forces from Angola. Indeed, the entire Third World—so important to Carter "on its merits"—was initially for Reagan just the stage on which the U.S.-Soviet struggle is played out, without much intrinsic importance and without the capacity to hurt the United States seriously.

As a result of such logic, the Reagan Administration has reversed most of its predecessor's policies in the Third World. It quickly scrapped the Carter arms-transfer restraints in favor of selling arms as a tool of influence, and it reduced the priority of nonproliferation efforts lest they alienate key American allies (like Pakistan) or cost the United States nuclear energy sales (for example, to China). Worrying about other people's human rights was seen by the first Reagan Administration as another luxury a threatened United States could ill afford, so it abandoned the public priority given to the issue in order to work with authoritarian regimes lest they be replaced by totalitarian ones in league with the Soviet Union. U.S. voluntary contributions to the UN system were reduced and Jeane Kirkpatrick was appointed ambassador to the UN to speak out forcefully against Third World abuse. Finally, the Administration sharply curtailed U.S. support for international financial institutions like the World Bank and the International Monetary Fund (IMF), considering them branches of the annoying UN system and a conduit for the taxpayers' funds to radical Third World regimes. Although all of these positions have softened during the second Reagan term, most of them remain fundamental parts of the Administration's political approach.

The Reagan Administration has thus been very clear about its allies and enemies, determined to replace the Carter Administration's moralistic affinity for the Third World with tangible rewards and punishments. Moreover, where Kissinger judged other countries on the basis of their foreign policy actions and not their form or philosophy of government, Reagan has included the internal structure and Marxist ideology of states like Nicaragua among the grounds for American opposition. Although the Administration made some tentative and intermittent efforts to reach accommodation with Marxist regimes in Mozambique, Angola and even Nicaragua, it has replied to their continuing recalcitrance with extraordinary pressure, boldly using a constellation of negative policy instruments to force them to cry "uncle." At the same time, Reagan has been much quicker than Carter to come to the support of Third World allies in a crisis, even with military aid, to show (as former Secretary of State Alexander M. Haig Jr. put it) that "a relationship with the United States brings dividends, not just risks." And the President has made it clear that U.S. support would extend to allied regimes challenged internally as well as those faced with external threats, that he would "not permit" Saudi Arabia, for example, to be a Nicaragua or an Iran: "...if we will make it plain...that we are going to stand by our friends and allies," he told the press in 1981, "I don't think... that kind of an overthrow will take place."

Such moves should not be taken to mean that the Reagan Administration has conducted a cold, calculating balance-of-power strategy on the Nixon-Kissinger model. On the contrary, the Administration's global security policy has been fired by ideological hostility, an attitude which has often put the U.S.S.R. and its clients beyond the pale of ordinary diplomacy. At the same time, the ideology of the right has provided an alternative structure of values to those pursued from the left by President Carter. The emphasis on human rights, nonproliferation and arms-transfer restraints has been replaced with major efforts to promote the ideology of capitalism and American-style democracy in the Third World. Speaking before the annual meetings of the World Bank and the IMF, for example, Reagan has consistently promoted capitalist economic policies and foreign investment as alternatives to foreign aid. The Administration has established the National Endowment for Democracy to promote elections and other parliamentary techniques of government overseas, and Reagan has even gone so far as to assist in the departure of authoritarian rulers from Haiti and the Philippines when their continuance in office seemed to threaten close U.S. security relationships with those countries. Finally, both the political and economic elements of the Administration's program have been backed by a renewed emphasis on propaganda, including major funding for the Voice of America and the establishment of new broadcast services like Radio Martí, aimed at Cuba.

Reagan's ideology has done more than provide the value structure for his Administration's foreign policy. It has also been a very important part of the President's leadership style, helping him master—in a way denied to Nixon or Carter—the post-Vietnam dissension in American public opinion. Where the Nixon Administration imposed its own conception on a divided nation and the Carter team embodied the country's confusion, Reagan provided a sense of direction—sold to the public via a contagious personal optimism and formidable communication skills.

For most of his presidency, this blend of ideology and political skill was very effective. Reagan pushed a dramatic redirection of American foreign policy through a national legislature half controlled by the opposing party. The defense budget was repeatedly raised (twice by double-digit percentages), security assistance was expanded at the expense of economic aid, covert actions and armed insurgencies against Soviet-backed regimes were funded, and the Strategic Defense Initiative was launched. Although sheer luck and the strong desire of Americans not to see another failed presidency have undoubtedly contributed to these accomplishments, Reagan has to be given much of the credit for his own success.

The Debt to the Future

As developments in the latter part of his presidency have shown, however, the Reagan leadership style is not without its drawbacks. The world is rarely as simple as ideology, whether of the right or left, portrays it. In the Iran-contra affair, for example, it was the President's ideological stance, combined with his detached management style and lack of detailed foreign affairs knowledge, that encouraged and allowed the foreign policy amateurs running the NSC staff to undertake operations that skirted both the law and the sensible boundaries of effective diplomacy. What made the scandal so damaging was precisely that it threw into question the very certainties that had commended the President to his countrymen, the assurances that the United States would never deal with terrorists, that Americans would no longer suffer humiliation at the hands of Iranian fanatics, and that the President himself was a man of integrity and conviction. But the environment which gave rise to the

Iran-contra affair was created much earlier, and the Reagan stewardship of foreign policy has much more serious and far-reaching implications than the mistakes made in this one policy area.

Indeed, the first Reagan Administration started off with ideological assumptions that gave a distorted view of the world, and as a result (much like Carter's) it had to back off from strongly articulated positions which proved unproductive. In the Middle East, the Administration found that all parties considered the Palestinian issue and the Arab-Israeli dispute far more important than the Soviet threat. So after a year and a half, strategic consensus had to be abandoned in favor of the September 1982 Reagan plan endorsing a Palestinian entity federated with Jordan. Similarly, by giving vent to neoconservative demands for renewed official relations with Taiwan, Washington almost did serious damage to the strategic relationship forged by Nixon and Carter with the People's Republic of China, only moderating that position in an August 1982 joint communiqué regulating arms sales to the island. In both cases, valuable time and American prestige were sacrificed by an obviously false start.

U.S.-Soviet Relations

The most serious impact of Reagan's ideology has been on U.S. policy toward the Soviet Union. Initially, American officials were so impressed with the inferiority of U.S. military power as to believe that no acceptable arms control treaty could be negotiated with Moscow. As a result, the President delayed serious bargaining until American rearmament was well under way, waiting nearly 18 months before beginning strategic arms reduction talks (START) and then tabling proposals which Secretary Haig considered clearly "unnegotiable." Meanwhile, Reagan's extremely tough talk about the Russians and his alarmingly candid discussions of nuclear war frightened his countrymen and allies, provided a major opening for Soviet propaganda, and energized a peace movement on two continents. Whether or not the Soviet Union ultimately proves willing to compromise, six years were lost before Administration officials seemed to change their views of the Kremlin in ways that may permit productive negotiations.

In many other areas, the Reagan ideological approach and basic worldview seem unable to embrace the contradictions which are an unavoidable part of the U.S. position in today's world. The Administration's stress on power, for example, might well create the conditions for a dramatically successful diplomacy; the use of power in one form or other is an essential part of any negotiation strategy. But with the Sandinistas as with the Soviets, the Administration seems to feel that negotiations are a process whereby the United States applies pressure and the other side capitulates, rather than a mutual search for compromise in which each side tries to define minimal objectives the other can accept. Given continuing domestic and international constraints on American power, it is an open question whether strong-arm tactics alone will succeed.

Moreover, if Carter's stress on the Third World and interdependence issues was ahead of its time, Reagan's bipolar preoccupation with the Soviet threat seems increasingly out of date. The Soviets do enjoy a certain quantitative military superiority. But real problems in the Third World also exist, problems that need to be addressed on their merits if only to provide less-fertile ground for Soviet penetration. And so do global and interdependence issues, which *can* compromise the U.S. national interest, if not endanger the country's survival. It may be, in fact, that an Administration concentrating on military power came into office just as forces making for the diffusion of power came into focus, that Reagan's bipolar worldview arrived just as Kissinger's pentagonal world is more than ever a possibility.

Policy Without Ambition

In fact, during the years of its apparent success as well as during its more recent discomfiture, the Reagan presidency may well have been doing a quiet disservice to the country it serves. Though the second Reagan Administration has moved toward the center and adopted a more pragmatic approach to foreign relations, it is still not clear that the President is ready to take risks in the vigorous pursuit of diplomatic objectives beyond the East-West struggle. Whereas Nixon advanced the restructuring of global geopolitics and Carter moved several outstanding political disputes toward resolution, Reagan so far lacks major foreign policy achievements. Perhaps a status quo policy is the best one can hope for in this era of reduced American power, and certainly protection of the nation's substantial assets is a President's first responsibility. But the Administration's very lack of diplomatic ambition may be causing the United States to ignore serious issues—in the Middle East, in southern Africa, in the arms race, and elsewhere—that could repay neglect with far-more-damaging impact in coming years.

Even the accomplishment of the Administration's first priority—the restoration of American power—is still in doubt. One cannot be sure that Reagan's efforts to restore the economy, rearm the military, revitalize U.S. alliances and reshape a domestic consensus will succeed in the long run. To be sure, the massive defense spending, tight monetary policies, and simultaneous tax cutting of first-term Reaganomics worked brilliantly to produce low-inflationary growth. But they have also generated massive Federal budget shortfalls, unprecedented trade deficits and a recession in manufacturing which could have serious long-term consequences for the very power base Reagan seeks to rebuild. Meanwhile, continuing lack of success in arms control may render the Reagan military buildup futile by loosening the legal and political restraints on Soviet weapons design and deployment. Finally, in the effort to rebuild American alliances, there is a danger that the Administration's downplaying of goals it considers peripheral (like human rights and nonproliferation) may eventually prove destructive of the very security relationships it was supposed to advance, as the Philippine case nearly proved, and South Korea, Pakistan or Zaire may yet show.

It is likely, in other words, that Kissinger and Carter were right, that broad, systemic changes in the international system have made a restoration of the predominance enjoyed by the United States during the 1950s impossible. At a minimum, the persistence of huge Federal budget deficits would seem to indicate a foreign policy in which ends have not been kept in proportion to means. Fiscal constraints have already begun to have a direct impact on the availability of foreign policy tools, stalling the expansion of military spending and drastically cutting foreign assistance budgets. Only time will tell whether the relative decline in American power can be reversed, as Reagan expects, rather than merely slowed and managed (as Kissinger thought) or welcomed and turned to advantage (as Carter believed). In the meantime, the debt to the future mounts steadily.

The Reagan Legacy

To raise such questions is not to imply, of course, that the Reagan foreign policy approach is bankrupt, whatever its implications for the solvency of American foreign relations. Like his predecessors, Reagan's broad legacy contains much that is positive, and any sustainable U.S. foreign policy will have to include many features that are indisputably his.

First among them is continuing attention to the sources of American power and a recognition of its inherently psychological nature. The decline of American power *was* in part American-made, and Reagan has shown that the United States can and must use its potential to create the necessary tools of foreign policy. He has also reminded us that the will to use those tools is important, that demonstration of vigorous leadership ready to defend American interests remains necessary in the international anarchy of today's world. *Possunt quia posse videntur*: They have power who seem to have power.

The second lesson to be drawn from the Reagan foreign policy is that, for the foreseeable future, the Soviet Union will continue to be at the center of American overseas concerns. Whether one sees the Soviets as "ruthless opportunists," like Kissinger, as people with whom one could achieve "mutual understanding," like Carter, or as an expanding "evil empire," like Reagan, they remain the only direct threat to American survival, and U.S.-Soviet diplomacy is the only interstate relationship where mistakes have the potential for destroying human life as we know it.

Though it is impossible to intimidate the Kremlin with American power and essential to deal with it on a broad range of nuclear and other issues, no Administration after Reagan's can entertain the illusion that Soviet-American relations can be based solely on cooperation or that any other set of issues can replace them as the paramount concern of U.S. statesmanship.

Finally, and most important, Reagan has highlighted both in failure and success the importance of foreign policy leadership in the post-Vietnam domestic context. The Nixon-Kissinger team knew what it was about in foreign affairs, but it did not persuade the American people and the Congress to accept a realistic vision of détente as an objective worthy of the United States. Carter embraced the diversity of American opinion about foreign relations and championed the idea of incorporating values in American diplomacy, but he could not lead public opinion forward to a new consensus because he lacked any overriding sense of the direction in which he wanted to go. Whatever the inadequacies of Reagan's vision or the shortcomings of his foreign policy management, his was the first presidency of the post-Vietnam era to combine a clear and principled approach with the leadership of public opinion necessary to get it across. The country will be well served if future Presidents not only inspire but also deserve such public confidence.

5

Public Opinion and the Policy Triangle

Two great intellectual traditions have contested in postwar U.S. foreign policy. The first, a legacy of the appeasement of Hitler at Munich and the cold war, holds that aggression must be resisted with strength and resolve; the second, springing in the post-Vietnam era from deep isolationist roots, warns that intervention is entangling and ends must be consistent with means. How can these traditions be combined in a coherent, sustainable policy that takes account of the actual U.S. power position without succumbing to historical pessimism; that sets policy goals in a framework of American values without embarking on ideological crusades; and that reflects geopolitical realities while responding to the democratic process?

The answer lies somewhere in the policy triangle sketched by the Nixon, Carter and Reagan Administrations. Drawing on the experience of the last two decades, it ought to be possible to lay out the rudiments of a sustainable policy for the post-Reagan era. If so, the place to begin is with public opinion.

The Developing Popular Consensus

The American people increasingly seem to think in a different way about foreign policy than the Administrations that we have described, according to Yankelovich. Where foreign affairs specialists tend to hold views that are highly structured and interrelated, the general public tends to pick and choose whatever policies seem most likely to work on a given issue without much concern for logical consistency. Concrete rather than abstract in his thinking, the man in the street doesn't worry if he is conservative on one issue and liberal on the next. Where policymakers' views may be ideological and politicized, people in general hold more centrist and moderate opinions. The people also tend to be more concerned with the ends than with the means of policy, probably because they have less experience with (and no vested interests in) the tools available to the policymaker to influence other nations. Moreover, ordinary individuals feel far more than the policymaker the impact of foreign policy decisions on everyday life. They know from experience that, in the end, they will be paying the bills for the policy community's mistakes.

Public opinion thus shows a range of views on foreign policy whose pragmatism and common sense sometimes seem to elude the specialist. Interestingly, the developing popular consensus reflects the dominant characteristics of each phase of post-Vietnam public opinion and echoes many of the positive elements in all three recent Administrations' foreign policy approaches. At the risk of overgeneralizing, here is what Americans seem to be saying to their government:

▶ Be cautious. Less activist than their leaders and mindful of the way costs seem always to escalate beyond projections and control, the people want to be sure that whatever is done is worth its cost and to defend what the nation has before embarking on grand adventures.

▶ Husband American resources. People are skeptical about the effectiveness of all policy tools and particularly reluctant to use American forces abroad. While a majority endorses economic aid in principle, bigger majorities want to cut spending on economic and military assistance.

▶ <u>Discriminate among interests</u>. The public insists *both* that vital interests be defended *and* that the government not make commitments in areas where critical national interests are not evident.

▶ <u>Contain and negotiate with the U.S.S.R.</u> The American people approve a tough posture toward the Soviet Union, but they also expect their government to do everything in its power to lessen tensions with Moscow and reach agreements to limit and control nuclear arms. Peace and strength are both obviously vital; they expect vigorous efforts in both directions.

▶ <u>Address new policy issues</u>. The people recognize that foreign policy must deal with more than just the Soviet threat. They expect their government to work with other nations to curb problems of global interdependence—within the cost and risk limitations described at the outset.

▶ <u>Promote economic self-interests</u>. Americans see economic objectives as a vital part of U.S. foreign policy. They expect government to help stimulate growth and productivity at home, ensure fair access to markets abroad, keep the value of the dollar steady and protect American jobs.

▶ <u>Project values where possible</u>. The public believes that American values must be a permanent part of U.S. foreign policy. But people do not want government to be altruistic. They will support the spread of democracy and capitalism abroad, but only to the extent it serves their interests at no great cost or sacrifice.

▶ <u>Be responsive and watch out</u>. Most Americans retain from the early post-Vietnam years a certain wariness regarding the actions of government. They will continue to be "skeptical, opinionated, critical [and] impatient, giving careful scrutiny to all initiatives," according to Yankelovich and Kaagan.

Of course, this brief litany should not imply that the American people hold unanimous views; public opinion is nothing if not contradictory. In fact, several in-depth studies of the post-Vietnam period highlight three basic trends within the overall consensus. First, internationalist opinion has branched into conservative and liberal wings, the one emphasizing military power to counter the overwhelming threat from an expansionist and revolutionary U.S.S.R., the other feeling that the Soviet threat is manageable through traditional diplomacy and that the U.S. should concentrate on nonmilitary dangers like economic issues

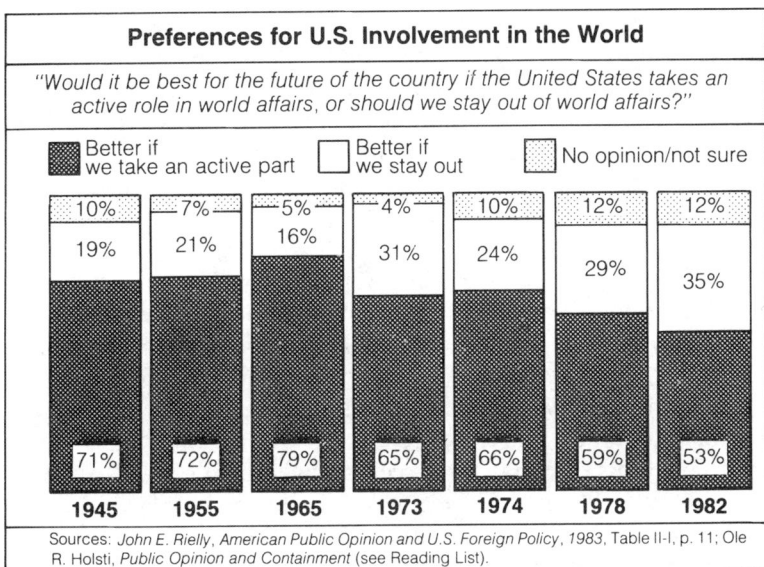

Sources: John E. Rielly, *American Public Opinion and U.S. Foreign Policy*, 1983, Table II-I, p. 11; Ole R. Holsti, *Public Opinion and Containment* (see Reading List).

and global interdependence. Second, a semi-isolationist or noninternationalist group has also emerged. With a strong focus on domestic priorities and with doubts about the success of many recent U.S. foreign policy endeavors, these people stress the limits on American resources and the need to restrict the goals of foreign policy accordingly. Third, there appears to be a renewed partisanship on many issues, with Republicans and Democrats holding opposite opinions on such matters as the presence of U.S. troops in South Korea, the U.S. role in El Salvador and Nicaragua, the dispatch of the Marines to Lebanon, and (recently) whether the defense budget is about right or should be cut.

These divisions hardly bode well for the kind of renewed consensus that a steady U.S. foreign policy needs. Still, it seems plausible that each of the post-Vietnam groups shares enough sympathy for the goals of the others to permit a working consensus among them. Most Americans share the conservative internationalists' respect for the power of the Soviet Union and want the United States to be strong enough to deal with it; most will go along with the liberal internationalist view that other foreign policy issues also need to be addressed by the U.S. government; but most people equally understand the new limits on American power and remain cautious and skeptical of foreign involvement. Given these overlapping concerns, it should not be impossible to outline a pragmatic policy that will be sustainable in the post-Reagan era.

The Elements of a Sustainable Policy

A viable post-Reagan foreign policy will have to be based on a series of apparent contradictions which spring from real-world conditions. Like Reagan's, a new policy will have to build the foundations of American power and pay attention to its psychological nature; but, like Kissinger's and Carter's, it will have to set aside any illusions that the predominance of the 1950s can be restored. It will need the clear-eyed, realistic view of the world held by the Nixon Administration, and will have to be pragmatic and centrist rather than sharply left or right. But it will also need some of the idealism and concern for American values characteristic of the Carter era, as well as the strong sense of direction imparted by Reagan in his first six years. It will have to be politically courageous and forward-looking like Carter, with a bold and definite agenda for action, and yet recognize that diplomatic progress is often measured in years or decades. And a sustainable post-Reagan policy will require both strong public leadership and sophisticated conceptual thinking, while remaining responsive to the democratic process.

What would such a policy look like? At its center would have to be a balanced approach to the Soviet Union that accepts with Kissinger and Nixon the imperatives of both containing Soviet expansion and preventing nuclear war. That kind of dual policy demands not only the application of power but the willingness to use diplomacy to lock in the gains power can secure. Given the awesome destructive potential of nuclear weapons, future Administrations need a tough-minded but genuine arms control policy, premised on the idea that partial and imperfect restraints on nuclear arms are better than unattainable visions of a nuclear-free world and that any stable yet progressive agreement must include real sacrifices on both sides. In other areas where the two countries have interests in common, the United States should try to move beyond propaganda to genuine exploration of those interests while remaining always ready to counter new Soviet transgressions.

A Pluralistic Policy

In the Third World, the United States must recognize the benefit of a favorable balance of power as a substitute for American preponderance of power. But it should not adopt Reagan's preoccupation with forging anti-Soviet coalitions there, nor need it contest like Nixon every ambiguous and marginal change in the balance lest it slip out of control forever. The nation's concern for avoiding nuclear war must restrain it from making every Third World crisis into an occasion for superpower confrontation and, while supporting its allies in the Third World, the country must understand that gradual shifts in American interests will necessitate occasional adjustments in its alliance structure.

In fact, the constraints on American power suggest that the United States should move gradually from an anti-Soviet to a pluralistic policy in the Third World. Though welcoming and supporting democratic and capitalist regimes abroad, Americans should never make a state's internal structure or policies the criteria for opposing it. Instead, the United States should emerge as the champion of a world of diversity, pointing out that only the Soviet Union demands ideological conformity. The harder, negative policy instruments should be applied only to states posing a clear danger to the United States. Finally, especially in areas where U.S. interests or leverage are not sizable, the United States should attempt to maximize its prestige and legitimacy by aligning itself with regional aspirations.

Such an approach would produce a Third World policy at once globalist and regionalist, powerful and conciliatory. In Central America, the United States would narrow its objectives to those achievable this side of military intervention, dropping its demands for democracy and the ouster of the Sandinista regime as the price for normalizing relations. It would offer instead to cease military pressure on Nicaragua in return for its binding promise to stop exporting revolution and not allow its territory to become a base for Soviet military power, making clear that it would take immediate military action against any violation of those pledges. In South Africa, the United States should adjust to the inevitability of black majority rule, acknowledging that constructive engagement has not and will not secure concessions from the white regime sufficient to justify the loss of American prestige it causes in black Africa. In the Middle East, the United States should move aggressively to build on the Camp David accords and the Reagan plan of 1982, opening informal dialogues with all parties having a role in a Palestinian settlement and working far more actively to defuse the political causes of terrorism.

Generally, the United States should be willing to talk to its opponents as well as its friends, using its power, like Reagan, to defend American interests, but willing like Carter to negotiate differences. While recognizing the continuing predominance of the bipolar security structure, it should understand that the world's economic and political system is moving fitfully toward a multipolar model, and that such movement is in the U.S. interest. A viable American foreign policy cannot afford to support a hundred allies any more than it can afford to oppose a hundred enemies; it must look favorably upon genuinely independent and nonaligned states as a positive element in the international system, rather than considering neutrality, as did Secretary of State John Foster Dulles, an "immoral and shortsighted conception."

Values and Interests

Such a policy would not at all mean the abandonment of American values. On the contrary, it would remain appropriate for the United States to deny material assistance and political support to nations which violate fundamental human rights and freedoms, just as it provides concrete help to those which share American political and economic values. But no future U.S.

Administration should assume like Jimmy Carter's that projecting American values abroad can take precedence over a foreign policy that protects U.S. prosperity and security at home.

Beyond such questions of values and politics, a post-Reagan foreign policy will have to address issues of self-interest, especially economic self-interest. Here Reagan's determination to revitalize the domestic economy must be matched by a Carter-like recognition of growing American economic interdependence. U.S. Presidents will be able to lead their people in the direction of free trade only if the government can help keep the country competitive without taking domestic economic actions that provoke foreign governments to shut out American products.

With all these demands and still-limited resources, will any room be left for addressing global issues? Perhaps, but only in the context of the public's self-interest. The United States will participate in efforts like the Law of the Sea negotiations only if its national interest is better served by being in than out. It will deal with global pollution to the extent that it is seen to be damaging the domestic ecology. And it seems unlikely that a sustainable U.S. foreign policy can seriously address broader issues of resource depletion and limits to growth until the scientific community can provide solid evidence of serious risk to the nation's prosperity or survival.

Can such a post-Reagan foreign policy be achieved? Is it possible to imagine a President who combines the competence and conceptual grasp of the Nixon-Kissinger team, the ambition, future-sight and focus on values possessed by Carter, and the sense of direction, political savvy and communication skills of Reagan? Will the climate of popular thought permit such a paragon to emerge and prosper in the years ahead? Though it would be foolish to predict such an outcome, the recentering of public opinion and the later pragmatism of both the Carter and Reagan Administrations offer considerable hope that the traditions of the cold war and Vietnam can be combined. Somewhere in the triangle of the Nixon, Carter and Reagan foreign policies, collective experience and common sense may yet find a new policy synthesis for the late 1980s and beyond. □

Talking It Over

A Note for Students and Discussion Groups

This issue of the HEADLINE SERIES, like its predecessors, is published for every serious reader, specialized or not, who takes an interest in the subject. Many of our readers will be in classrooms, seminars or community discussion groups. Particularly with them in mind, we present below some discussion questions—suggested as a starting point only—and references for further reading.

Discussion Questions

Should Americans expect that the predominance enjoyed by the United States during the cold-war years can be restored by wise management of the country's resources, or is it unlikely that the underlying systemic trends making for the relative decline of American power can be overcome?

Can the U.S. government deal with the relative decline of the nation's power by resisting and disguising it, paying careful attention to the psychological nature of power, or should the United States narrow its objectives and limit its responsibilities by a careful balancing of ends and means? Is the balance of power a useful tool of foreign policy for the coming years, or will the United States be able to redefine its interests in ways that turn the current American power position to advantage?

What degree and kind of threat does the Soviet Union pose to American national security? In what areas should the United States compromise with the U.S.S.R., and how much are the American people willing to pay in arms costs and risk of war to protect those interests they deem essential?

How important a role should economic and Third World issues play in U.S. foreign policy? What sacrifice in self-interest are Americans willing to make to pursue traditional values in their foreign relations?

Does the nation need to follow a broadly active foreign policy, spending its resources and risking its prestige in attempts to settle difficult international conflicts, manage economic interdependence, treat global issues, and deal with other threats to world peace and order? Or can it focus more directly on problems at home than it has in recent years?

Do Americans want an open, democratic and responsive Administration, in spite of the inefficiencies and incoherence that may introduce into American foreign policy? Or are they willing to settle for broad electoral control, delegating the specifics of policy to professionals at the cost of occasional moral or even constitutional lapses?

READING LIST

Memoirs

Brzezinski, Zbigniew, *Power and Principle: Memoirs of the National Security Advisor, 1977-1981.* New York, Farrar, Straus, Giroux, 1983.

Carter, Jimmy, *Keeping Faith: Memoirs of a President.* New York, Bantam Books, 1982.

Haig, Alexander M., Jr., *Caveat: Realism, Reagan, and Foreign Policy.* New York, Macmillan, 1984.

Kissinger, Henry, *White House Years*. Boston, Mass., Little, Brown, 1979.

———, *Years of Upheaval*. Boston, Mass., Little, Brown, 1982.

Nixon, Richard, *RN: The Memoirs of Richard Nixon*. New York, Grosset & Dunlap, 1978.

Vance, Cyrus, *Hard Choices: Critical Years in America's Foreign Policy*. New York, Simon and Schuster, 1983.

Analyses

Bell, Coral, "From Carter to Reagan." *Foreign Affairs* (America and the World 1984), Vol. 63, No. 3.

Brown, Seyom, *The Faces of Power: Constancy and Change in United States Foreign Policy from Truman to Reagan*. New York, Columbia University Press, 1983.

Deibel, Terry L., "Why Reagan Is Strong." *Foreign Policy*, Spring 1986.

Gaddis, John Lewis, *Strategies of Containment: A Critical Appraisal of Postwar American National Security Policy*. New York, Oxford University Press, 1982.

Gelb, Leslie H., "Reagan, Power, and the World." *The New York Times Magazine*, November 13, 1983. See also "The Mind of the President." *The New York Times Magazine*, October 6, 1985.

Holsti, Ole R., "Public Opinion and Containment," in Terry L. Deibel and John Lewis Gaddis, eds., *Containing the Soviet Union*. New York, Pergamon-Brassey's, 1987.

Nye, Joseph S., Jr., "U.S. Power and Reagan Policy." *Orbis*, Summer 1982.

Rielly, John E., *American Public Opinion and U.S. Foreign Policy 1983*. Chicago, Ill., Chicago Council on Foreign Relations, 1983. See also 1979 and 1987 reports.

Tucker, Robert W., "The Purposes of American Power." *Foreign Affairs*, Winter 1980/81.

Yankelovich, Daniel, and Kaagan, Larry, "Assertive America." *Foreign Affairs* (America and the World 1980), Vol. 59, No. 3.